What workshop and retre

"There's no dogma, no superiority, no guru-ness, no rigid mindset, no rules, just a loving intelligence continually welcoming us back to the home we never left."
– P C

"James is a born teacher—infinitely patient, compassionate, crystal clear and with great integrity. Thank you James, for your wisdom and love."
– L P

"I am a different person since working with James: more real, more loving, more open, more joyous, and certainly much more alive! People remark on it."
– J B

"I am very glad that Life has brought me to you. Your words and presence had a profound impact on me. After years in a kind of impasse/wilderness I am now filled with joy, with peace."
– L W

"James's teachings are clear and concise. They took me to a level of understanding that had eluded me for 45 years. A truly life changing experience that opened a new possibility for being alive."
– C L

"Thank you James. You act as a midwife, guiding and supporting us through the pangs and contractions of giving birth to our true selves!"
– M W

"The first time I connected with James it was a life-changing epiphany; to totally meet and be met on a transpersonal level— it was literally awesome. This is all I have ever wanted, and I am so grateful that the universe introduced me to someone I resonate with and learn so much from."
– M J

"Working closely with a guide who knows the territory, who can understand where we are on the journey, who meets us and sees us as we really are and reflects that back to us, is a rare and precious opportunity. James is that very guide."
– J B

"Thank you dear James. I've heard the words so many times and no one has ever led me to a place where I could actually experience those words—like what does it mean? That's what I was asking for, and you managed to do it."
– A B

Daring
to Burn

Collected Essays on Exploring Reality
and Finding the Courage to Feel
the Fullness of Life

James Eaton

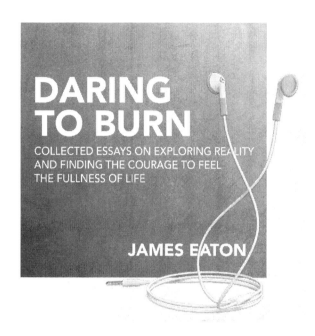

Download the Audiobook for Free!

As a big thank you for buying my book I'd like to give you the Audiobook version for free.

To Download Go To:

https://jameseaton.org/daring-to-burn/audiobook

Acknowledgments

For reading through the original essays, and helping me to choose the most suitable for this collection, I'm deeply grateful to Eleonora Russo, Clive Buckland-Bork, Matthew Eatwell, Lynton Davidson, Lucie Petrides and Jitindriya Bell.

Big-hearted thanks to my editor and proofreader, Susan Turner, for offering so many helpful comments and suggestions.

Love and gratitude to my many teachers, and to all those who have attended a workshop, retreat or individual session with me—through your courageous sharing and challenging questions I have learned so much.

Most of all I thank the greatest teacher of all, life itself, for this extraordinary ride.

For my sweet love Eleonora,
and our two little wonders
Edward and Ludo.

Contents

Introduction...1

PART 1: 2013

The Miracle of Love...9
Has Nothing Ever Happened?...............................11
The Ultimate Healing...13
Snakes and Ladders...15
Fear..18
God's Brain...21
River of Love..24
Waiting 26
Is This It?..29
The Promised Land...32
The Prodigal Son..35
Deep Honesty..39
Christmas with the Relatives.................................42

PART 2: 2014

The Real Story..47
Smiling Buddha...50
Piranhas..53
The Last Crusade...54
Blown Apart...58
Daring to Burn..59
The Complete Sandwich...62

The Real Signalman...63

The Cycle of Criticism...64

The Cosmic X-Ray...67

Dear Parents Everywhere, I Salute You!.................68

"Calm Down"..69

Doing the Dishes..71

Innocent Eyes..72

Life Purpose...73

Black Mood...74

Jigsaw Puzzle..75

Telling the Truth...77

Flip-Flop..78

Comparisons...79

Double Bind..80

Origami...81

'To Do' Lists...84

The Fool..86

Hidden Agendas...88

Beyond 'Mindfulness'...90

What is Happiness?...93

Feedback Loop...95

The Visceral Throb...97

PART 3: 2015

Who is with You Now?...101

Beyond the Skin...102

The Escape Artist...104

Molten Lava..106

The Greatest Show On Earthlessness...................107

Sacred Digestion...109

Game of Seduction...110

Enjoying the Party...112

One Taste..114

Monopoly..117

PART 4: 2016

Blossoming into Life...121

The Real Fireworks...123

The Most Glorious Song of All......................................125

Waking Up from Waking Up..127

Introduction

The collection of essays that form this book were written between 2013 and 2016 in response to themes that arose in my workshops and retreats, as well as in my own life, during that time. When gathering the writings together it became clear to me that, to get the most value out of the book, an introduction would be required to provide context for understanding the essays that follow. So here is that very introduction, which is similar to what I offer at the beginning of each of my workshops and retreats.

The fundamental belief in our culture is that each of us is exclusively a separate subject, moving through an independently existing world full of objects and other subjects. With that belief installed we go out into the world to live our lives. However, at some point, many of us begin to notice that, whatever we acquire or achieve in life, there is this underlying sense of something missing and the longing for more—that doesn't go away. We may spend our whole life trying to find the right partner, career, place to live, country to live in etc. etc. but, however much we change the furniture of our lives, that sense of lack and longing for more persists—like a hunger that just can't be satisfied.

So what do we do? We may try to avoid facing the issue with a whole range of compulsions, from over working and general busyness to using drugs, alcohol, food, shopping and so on; or else we continue going round in circles trying to fix 'the problem', becoming ever more disillusioned as we see that ultimately nothing seems to work and there's no way out of the loop.

So where do we go from here? Thankfully there is another way! We begin to question that fundamental belief upon which all our subsequent activity is based: that what I am is exclusively a separate subject, divided off from the world, from objects and other subjects.

So how do we do that? We don't need to have read certain books or studied particular ideas, or to have had any previous experience even. All we need is *this* experience right now; and here it is! We allow ourself to put to one side all our sophisticated adult knowledge and become very simple, innocent and childlike. And in letting go of all our concepts and assumptions, what can we say with absolute certainty about this *immediate* experience now?

Whatever we are, whatever that is, IS. Here it is. And whatever it is that we are, seems to have this quality of knowing, or being aware—is aware of these words on the page, the sounds and smells of the environment, the feelings and sensations in the body plus whatever thoughts are appearing. And as those 'external' sounds and smells change, whatever we are doesn't—it remains as it is, aware of the changing experience. So whatever we are cannot be made of a sound or a smell. Similarly as those 'internal' feelings, body sensations and thoughts change, whatever we are doesn't—it is simply here, being aware of the changing experience. So whatever we are cannot be made of a feeling, body sensation or thought either.

When we look, in this childlike way, at our *actual* experience, it appears that what we are is pure awareness or knowing, that cannot have any objective qualities—no size, shape, colour, thickness, etc.—because by definition it is what is aware *of* those qualities, and so cannot *be* those qualities.

This realisation is profound, since it dissolves the belief that we are 'inside' the body, usually behind the eyes looking out, and instead we discover the body to be appearing to us, awareness, as equally as everything else. However, the sense of longing still persists. Why? Because we, as awareness, still feel separate from life; there is still a duality between pure knowing and experiencing.

How do we resolve that? Having explored the nature of ourself as subject, we now look more deeply into the nature of objects. And, rather than a world of independently existing forms, we discover a vibrant cocktail of perceptions. Our experiential reality is made out of a collection of colours, sounds, smells, tastes, feelings, sensations and thoughts, that all mix together in infinitely many combinations to create the 'as if' appearance of life happening—a kind of virtual reality. Really understanding this is crucial to taking the step we're about to take.

So far we have gone from what I'll call the 'conceptual view'—that we are separate subjects moving through an independently existing objective world; to the 'experiential view'—that we are pure awareness, experiencing a flow of perceptions. Now, take any of those perceptions, for example whatever sound is currently appearing. From the 'experiential view', awareness is experiencing a spontaneously arising sound (closing the eyes can be helpful in appreciating this).

But can we measure a gap between awareness and the arising sound? Where is awareness? Where do we begin our measurement? And can we find a boundary between awareness and the sound? Where is the edge of awareness?

As we start to ask these unusual questions that we may never have even contemplated before, we begin to recognise something extraordinary: that the awareness we truly are is *indivisible* from our experience; that awareness is *being* the experience, is *being* life itself. This is the miraculous realisation that brings an end to all the longing. What we really are is already whole, already complete. Nothing was ever truly missing. Our longing was like an intelligent messenger, letting us know that we were overlooking the wonder of our essential nature.

This is what the term non-duality means—that truly there are not two things, but simply the wholeness of *being*.

With that realisation we don't lose the 'conceptual view'; we can still use all our useful labels and concepts to frame reality. However in seeing beyond them we can now hold them lightly, and not take them as the literal 'truth' of things. Then they no longer lock us up inside a conceptual prison, including the prison of being exclusively incarcerated inside a body.

This understanding is the beginning of a very beautiful journey of unfolding. In recognising the true ground of being, all the coping mechanisms that we've developed over a lifetime can now begin to unravel. It's in that deep release that our unique character can begin to truly shine into life, unconstrained by the need to present some idea of how we 'should' be, in order to earn love and acceptance.

Phew! It's tricky to cram it all in to just a few pages. If you'd like to explore the nature of reality further, then I have a series of online courses that go into much greater depth, that will soon be available via my website: www.jameseaton.org.

With much love and warm wishes,

James Eaton
March 2018

PART 1: 2013

The Miracle of Love

Laughing with friends, playing together with children, walking in nature, making love, experiencing a beautiful piece of music, a film or work of art—these are just a few of the countless moments in all our lives when the utter conviction that we are a limited, isolated self, separated off from the rest of the world, can dissolve away.

And then there is the birth of a child. I look now adoringly at our newborn son, caress his delicate, soft skin, gaze into his endless eyes, see his precious little form cradled in his mother's arms, who, after the pain, the agony and the torment of labor, is now radiant with joy, our other, two year old son at her side. With the profound beauty of it all there is only love. Love of such power, such intensity, that any attempt to contain it or divide it is simply blown away.

Often we view these moments as special events or unusual occurrences that stand apart from the ordinariness of our everyday reality. But what if the exact opposite were true? What if these moments offer a glimpse of our real, abiding nature, shining unobscured, before our structure of definitions reassembles itself and, in being believed in, clouds the view once more?

Then these timeless moments come as an invitation, a catalyst, to deeply explore how life is beyond our thought-made interpretation; to unveil our true nature, the ultimate mother, whose infinitely fertile womb gives birth to this ever fresh experience called life—to every sound, image, sensation, taste, smell, thought and feeling; to time, space, colour and form; to this entire body of experiencing—without ever being separate from it.

Then we see that we *are* the laughter *and* our friends, we *are* the children we play together with, the lover and the loved, this text on the page and the message of freedom that it conveys. And yes, so too are we those powerful feelings that thought labels as 'unwanted' and tries its hardest to resist for fear of being destroyed. And yes, even those thoughts too, still hung up on the old belief that we are exclusively an isolated, vulnerable little 'me'.

Whatever is in experience can never *not* be what we are. That is the pure intimacy for which we long. That is coming home. That is the miracle of love.

Has Nothing Ever Happened?

A friend once went to a post Christmas non-duality meeting and was told that Christmas had never happened. This caused him much confusion as he still had the presents to prove that it had! So what on earth is going on here?

Statements such as 'nothing has ever happened' can be useful in smashing through the conviction that we understand life. They put such a spanner in the works that we are caused to reflect on all of our assumptions. However they can also be downright confusing at the same time! Thought is such a tricky customer that, rather than being undermined by these statements, it twists them to further reinforce its own supposed position as master controller. We can find ourselves becoming detached from life, as if it's some kind of meaningless mirage, which we, in our 'superior spiritual space', have now transcended beyond. We start telling others about what we know, and are extra careful so as not to use the 'wrong' language and so reveal a weakness in our ever thickening defensive wall. But all we have done is taken on another belief. This cold, intellectual non-duality is a million miles a way from what the message is really saying.

If we imagine ourself to be like a TV screen out of which the movie of life is made, then yes, nothing ever happens. Does the screen ever go anywhere? Does it ever change in any way whatsoever or have anything to say about anything? Is it affected when the movie is full of explosions? Of course not.

BUT!!! there *is* a movie playing out and that movie is *made out of* the screen. Every appearance is ourself in disguise, a manifestation of our true being. So to reject any aspect of the movie is to reject ourself.

Rather we find a raw intimacy with *all* of experiencing; be it our family, friends or a passing stranger; be it a feeling of joy, sadness or total frustration; be it a quiet walk in nature, the chaotic January sales or the local Christmas panto, everyone and everything is seen as an expression of who we truly are— all arising within the screen whilst never being separate from it.

Then this message goes from being a cold, intellectual appreciation to cracking open the heart and the love just pours out. Love without cause, love without reason.

So, did Christmas ever happen?

Oh no it didn't . . . Oh yes it did!

The Ultimate Healing

There is an idea that freedom is the grand prize for having healed all psychological wounds, dissolved all conditioning, and worked through all 'negative' patterns of behaviour. But is that really what freedom is?

Working on oneself in this way can of course be beneficial in bringing more well-being into one's life. But we can easily become caught in a cycle of longing for some future moment of perfection, and so completely miss the wonder that is shining as *this* moment.

True freedom is always already available, whatever our 'condition'. When we let go of all our ideas, beliefs and concepts to which we cling so tenaciously—our name, age, gender, ethnicity, nationality, occupation, political beliefs, religious beliefs, all of our roles and self images, all our hopes, dreams and desires—and stand 'here' stripped bare with nothing left to hold, then, to our utter amazement, rather than falling dead to the floor our heart leaps for joy! Without our prison of definitions there is nothing to separate a 'you' from a 'me' from a 'this' from a 'that' and we feel vividly alive.

This is the crucifixion and the resurrection. "Whoever will lose his life shall find it," says Jesus. These words you are now reading, the intimate thought that reflects upon them, the tingling sensations in your toes, the sound of traffic, the smell of coffee, the man walking by with his dog, the image of the sky—*all* are equally an expression of who you truly are.

This is not a rejection of life: on the contrary. When we see that nothing can threaten or contain our essential nature, all is welcome. And that *includes* our world of definitions too, as well as feelings of fear, anxiety, sadness and discomfort. Even resistance to that welcoming and the sense of contracting back down into a limited 'me' is also welcome!

The paradox is (and isn't there always a paradox) that as a by-product of this openness, this total immersion, this unconditional honouring of life, there *can* be a transformation, there *can* be falling away of the patterns and activities that require the belief in the separate 'me' for their lifeblood. This is the ultimate healing.

Then, just as the rising sun dissolves the shadows of the night, this understanding gradually spreads into all areas of our experience, ever deepening, ever enlightening, ever celebrating this wondrous miracle of being.

Snakes and Ladders

Out of our deep longing for something more, many of us find ourselves drawn into the bustling market of self-improvement and spirituality. Maybe we try to cultivate positivity and aspire to become a brighter, healthier, more present 'me'; or maybe we hear about wonderful transcendental experiences, spiritual fireworks, colourful lights, auras, the paranormal, and we go looking for those mystical delights, go looking for a permanent experience of peace, love and happiness, and for a time it may seem to work.

But, inevitably, we cannot maintain our newly imposed structure of 'shoulds' and 'shouldn'ts', and whatever big experiences we have fade. Then we beat ourselves up for not getting it 'right', for having missed some vital piece of information, or else we live in denial of our 'failure'. Either way our longing remains as we're still locked inside a mesh of thinking, still trying to get 'there'.

We may read all the books, the Facebook posts, watch the YouTube clips, go to the workshops and retreats, but the frustration grows as the harder we try the craftier thought seems to become. We hear the message that there are no positions to take, and thought cleverly takes the position of taking no positions. Someone gently suggests that we stop judging, and thought immediately begins judging our judging. Another kindly soul advises us to just 'accept what is' and off thought runs again busily working on accepting, and certainly not accepting the moments when life is so painful that it simply can't be accepted. We observe those that seem to have 'got it' and compare ourselves to them, maybe even trying to model their behaviour. "Stop trying so hard" they may cry, and so we try to stop trying!

Even when thought seems to lose its bewitching power and there is a glimpse of the full, rich, vibrancy of life, thought jumps up again with "I've finally got it!" and engages itself with the task of trying to work out exactly what it has 'got' so as not to lose it, and alas we're seemingly lost again.

What an exhausting game of snakes and ladders!

Thought is continually trying it on, continually reasserting its importance by negotiating with life as if it were the one in charge. As a last resort we decide it's up to 'grace' and that there's nothing 'I' can do, and so we work really hard at *doing* doing nothing—*anything* to create some framework to life; *anything* to avoid the sheer terror of having nothing left to hold.

Of course, thought can't decide to stop believing in thought any more than we can decide tomorrow's weather. That's just more of the same game; and thought trying to not believe itself is a real recipe for confusion! However, all this seeking, all this exploring is such a precious gift. We start to see the mechanism of thought and how it operates; we notice that, as thought dissolves, what we truly are is still here, still alive, still shining. How could thought ever understand THAT within which it arises and dissolves? You can't jump over your own knees!

And, as we become more and more familiar with life beyond thinking, our investment in our ideas, beliefs and concepts naturally softens, our attachment to our definitions naturally relaxes. Then there is nothing to split this-experience-now into pieces—no edges, no borders, no you, me, this or that, no beginning and no end—just open, undivided being; utterly simple, utterly effortless; the home we always longed for, the freedom we always craved, the lover whose arms we yearned to dissolve in.

Then thought can think what it likes. It's not our enemy. We are thought too and can marvel at its ingenious creativity. But when it comes to who we truly are, thought is deeply deluded. It believes that we're exclusively a limited, fragile little entity, under threat from the 'outside world'. All of its positioning and repositioning comes as an honest attempt to find safety and security—to survive.

But now we can enjoy the joke as thought hatches its latest rescue plan; enjoy the laughter at the sheer wonderment of it all. There never was anything to get right or wrong, or anywhere to get *to*. The 'there' we'd been longing to find is 'here' and always was; but now we know it once more, like we've never known it before.

Fear

Fear is very useful. That sudden pounding of the heart, tightening of the muscles and quickening of the breath lets us know we're in physical danger, stops us walking into oncoming traffic or falling off the edge of a cliff; it can even provide us with tremendous amounts of energy to help save ourself, or others, in a life threatening situation. But there is another kind of fear: the fear of the future, the fear of the past, the fear of being caught out, of what other people might think, of being judged, blamed or humiliated, of being the one who doesn't know, the one who got left behind, the one who got it 'wrong'.

This 'psychological' fear wreaks havoc with our lives creating all kinds of mental, physical and emotional stress. And for what? There is no *actual* physical danger here: no hungry lion bounding towards us or venomous snake poised to strike. This sense of threat that causes the heart to race and the body to tense is entirely made-up, existing only in the abstract realm of thought—our world of make-believe. We have become so completely fixated on our *idea* of who we are—that fleeting bundle of self images we call 'me'—that we mis-take this thought-made imposter for our very lifeblood. Whenever that *idea* is challenged, it's as if we literally *are* in physical danger. To be defeated or fail in our attempt to escape means death; and death is what we fear most of all.

And so the game goes on. Each time the latest version of the 'me' story is challenged, up jumps fear again along with its gang of unwanted stress and anxiety. Maybe we become aggressive and fight against whoever or whatever creates the threat; or we live in denial, trying to suppress or control those turbulent feelings; or we live small, retreating to the sidelines of life in an attempt to hide away from any potential future conflict. Either way we resist the discomfort, fleeing back into our conceptual world for reassurance, immersing ourself in our routines—our work, TV, hobbies, moral beliefs, religious beliefs, spiritual beliefs—*anything* to reinforce the sense that we are in control, that we know, until inevitably we're challenged once more and round we go again!

Maybe we spend our whole life on the run from fear, or maybe there comes a moment when, utterly exhausted with trying to maintain the charade, with trying to protect our fragile house of cards from every blow of air, every rock of the table, we're finally ready to stop all the pretending, to give our 'self' up to the fear and let it consume us entirely.

And in that furnace of truth, as the myths explode and all the divisions melt away, we come to know a depth of being beyond imagination, beyond comprehension.

What a revelation: the death of all resistance is the birth of boundless love!

When we know ourself as THAT, we no longer look to the fictional me and its story for our identity, we are set free from the cycle—free to really feel the full intensity of those energies we label as stress, anxiety, humiliation; free to allow them to finally release; free for our unique character to shine more than ever before. Then fear no longer comes as an enemy to be denied, suppressed or escaped, but as a welcome friend, an honest teacher, revealing and melting away the residues of the outdated *mis*understanding that what we are is a separate 'inside' self cut off from a separate 'outside' world.

Without the fear of fear itself, life opens up and Love courses through the veins of our true body, this moment, and *all* that it contains; nourishing and healing, bringing joy and aliveness to this ever-fresh, magical play of existence.

God's Brain

Within the beautiful grounds of Dartington Hall in Devon sits a spherical stone sculpture, over a metre high, of 12 spirals. Once, whilst walking nearby, I overheard a conversation between a young boy and his mum: "What's that mum?" asked the boy pointing to the sculpture. "What do you think it is?" she said. After a short pause for thought he replied earnestly, "Is it God's brain?" A perfectly reasonable reply I thought, if you've learnt to believe that God is a big old man with a white beard who lives in the sky.

As we grow older we may upgrade our idea of what God is, or perhaps abandon our ideas altogether and become a complete atheist. But whatever our version of 'the truth' is, whether we view life through the prism of religion, spirituality, science, or a combination of them all, *we are still looking through a conceptual prism*, still inhabiting a thought-made model of belief, and no model, however sophisticated or refined, is ever the living reality.

Of course thought is a very useful tool. This rich language we use to express our thoughts and feelings, the numbers we use to quantify and calculate, the ingenious concepts involved in the cutting edge of science and technology are all born of the inventiveness of thought. But thought looking for who we really are is like a character in a movie searching for the screen on which it appears, or the hero in a novel looking for the paper upon which the story is written—it's not difficult, it's impossible.

The idea of going beyond thought, beyond belief, of free falling into uncertainty, into the unknown, of being totally exposed and vulnerable with nothing left to hold, is commonly viewed as the road to ruin, madness and oblivion.

But what if we're wrong? What if we *can* go beyond thought, beyond belief, and not be destroyed? What if we *can* drop all the conceptual prisms and find we're still here, still breathing, still alive?

Then, without those thought-made partitions, this effortless, self-evident sense of being is revealed to be undivided from all of experience, is *being* all of experience—is being the thought that is now considering this statement, the movement and sound of every breath, every sensation, is being this page, the text upon it, and even the idea of a separate 'me' that is reading it. All are unique permutations of colour, sound, sensation, taste, smell, thought and feeling, all arising and dissolving in, and only ever made out of ourself—"the baseless fabric of this vision" as Shakespeare puts it.

To know oneself as 'all that is', to be fully immersed in life, saturated with all the joy, bliss, heartache and pain, the triumphs and the disasters, the satisfaction and the crushing disappointment, to feel it *all*, in all its bittersweet glory, is the essence of love.

And as that love radiates throughout our life, there comes a natural movement to cherish our relationships, cherish our communities, cherish and celebrate each and every expression of what we truly are—the transformational power of love becomes our living reality.

It turns out that the sculpture at Dartington Hall is entitled 'Jacob's Pillow', named after the biblical figure who, sleeping with his head on a stone, dreamed of a ladder reaching from heaven down to the earth. On awaking from the dream Jacob exclaims, "*This* is none other than the house of God!" A statement of pure non-duality! The ladder bridges the seeming 'gap', revealing that there really is no separation, no split.

Such is the original meaning of the word religion—to reconnect with that which has seemingly been lost, the coming together of heaven and earth, the holy consummation.

Given the nature of Jacob's dream, and the fact that the sculpture's 12 spirals represent the 12 apostles, commissioned by Jesus to spread his teaching, it seems the boy's idea of 'God's brain' was truly inspired.

River of Love

When the tensions build in our relationships, when we find ourselves being offhand and unresponsive, when we finally explode and argue with our loved ones—to prove that it's their fault and never our own, that they are in the wrong, that we are the victim—is this the beginning of the end or another invitation to go ever deeper?

This bunch of thoughts and feelings that have usurped our identity needs to be right; to be wrong is to be utterly humiliated, a kind of a death. But who we really are has nothing to fear, no need to be right, no image to uphold or protect. We are like the page on which these words appear; that gives them their substance, their very reality; that remains as it is, whatever drama the story may express.

As that deep recognition, like a healing balm, seeps into all areas of our life, a new possibility opens up: the possibility to see some truth in what we're being told, to see exactly where we're still pretending, where we still misunderstand, where we're still rejecting 'uncomfortable' feelings and wanting life to be different to the way it is.

How incredible, how inspiring, in the heat of battle to see our mis-take, to lay down our weapons and offer our heart; to fully embrace the energy of the moment as it incinerates all positions, all protection, all boundaries between 'me' and 'you' leaving us wide open.

And in that openness, that pure intimacy, to see my true face in your face, my true eyes in your eyes, and our troubles dissolve away like rain drops on a river of love.

Waiting . . .

Often we find ourself waiting in life: to finish work, for our holidays, for retirement, for the warmer weather to come, to meet the right partner, for our 'flaws' to be fixed, to be free of all conditioning, for the epiphany of realising the truth of who we really are . . . waiting for the end of all the waiting.

And so we live in expectation. Expectation of some future moment of fulfilment, thereby making *this* moment inferior and lacking—a stepping stone to somewhere else—or maybe so painful, ugly or terrifying that it is in desperate need of escaping.

We can spend a lifetime in waiting, convinced that happiness lies under the next stone, around the next corner, over the brow of the next hill; or maybe we start to notice that the waiting never ends, that the goal posts are continually moving, that whenever we do finally get what we think we want, the moment of satisfaction is only ever fleeting, before we become caught in some new cycle of longing and take our seat once more in the waiting room of life.

In recognising the utter futility of it all—that it's the belief that life is 'elsewhere' which creates the very anxiety, tension and stress we long to be rid of—we may be willing to look again at this insufficient present moment; to deeply explore what lies beneath the labels 'boredom', 'discomfort', 'sadness' and 'fear', before they're packaged up and pushed away as unwanted.

And what do we find when we really *feel* it?

We feel tingling, pulsing, throbbing sensations, a vibrant, energetic aliveness, the electricity of life; forces moving, resisting and opening, aching and softening, flowing unpredictably like a current of air from a playful breeze to a chaotic, rampaging tornado, dancing with light, floating steps, then suddenly punchy and intense; colours, shapes, smells and tastes, sounds, silences, heating and cooling—an immediate, compelling and utterly captivating 'happening'.

This is the rich, living vitality that we become numb to, that is continually rejected in favour of an idea—an abstract, untouchable, unfeelable idea of how it all 'should' be.

And what of this insufficient 'me'? The one that should be happier, fitter, brighter, sexier, more spiritual, more 'awake'?

Beyond all our judgments about what's right and wrong there's beauty in our flaws and our frailties, grace in our kooky, dippy, awkwardness, wonder in all our tender, delicate humanness—that particular way we look, that particular way we walk and talk—*all* of it, *including* the 'imperfections', going into the make of our unparalleled uniqueness; a human work of art, sculpted and fired by the most talented, prolific artist unimaginable.

We don't have to be superman or superwoman, don't have to be anyone else or anywhere else. We can simply be who we already are, here and now, what a relief! Does a tree ever wish it were taller, had different shaped leaves or grew in a different part of the forest? How absurd!

Of course this doesn't mean we can't make plans, expand our knowledge, develop our talents or try to achieve things in life, if that's where we find our joy. It's when we believe we need to do these things *in order to earn love and acceptance* that the suffering begins. And neither do we have to start sleeping on a bed of nails, wearing a hair-shirt or a spiked chain around our thigh to feel the moment more intensely! Oh how we love to make it all so difficult, so epic and heroic.

In feeling that easiness, that deep ok-ness with life *as it is*, the protective layers can begin to loosen; and as the costumes fall and the masks all drop, here, in our nakedness, exposed and vulnerable, feeling the raw, fragile, heart-aching beauty of our humanity, we come to know the incomprehensible miracle of our divinity.

To know the essence of our being, the lifeblood of all experiencing, that is what all the longing is truly for, what all the pain, fear and discomfort is continually beckoning us towards. And in that delicious homecoming lies the end of all the waiting.

So what are you waiting for?

Is This It?

"So this is it? So what." said a man bluntly at the beginning of one of my meetings.

As we began exploring together it became clear that he had long understood the notion of Wholeness—that life is truly undivided—but deep in his heart he still felt separate and isolated, yearning for a deeper connection with others, with life, longing for love, longing to come home, longing to come alive. The anger and resentment he felt was for a lifetime of seeking; a lifetime of spiritual paths, books, videos, teachers and practices; a lifetime spent craving some great epiphany, some permanent transcendent experience which frustratingly continued to elude him.

But what if what we long for doesn't need to look a certain way, and doesn't need to be attained or developed? What if the anger and resentment, the frustration, worry and anxiety, are all equally as valid an expression of life as the peace, joy and bliss? What if it's the very looking for some special state, for some extra add-on to life, that continually blinds us from the sheer obviousness of it all?

When we no longer try to deny, distract or escape, we find ourself *here*, with nowhere left to turn, and the invitation then is to *feel* whatever arises—to soften into the anger, the fear, the sense of deficiency and lack. It's in that absolute opening to life that the real miracle takes place. Life absorbs 'us' into its arms, and in that infinite embrace, that total merging, the Wholeness of being is all that remains.

In opening to our human fragility, we discover our invincibility.

Then our sense of vulnerability no longer need be resisted or denied, for who we really are has nothing to fear. Does the sky fear the crack of thunder and stroke of lightening of a passing storm? Does the screen fear whatever scene of horror its pixels give expression to? Then Wholeness, this Knowing beyond understanding, is no longer an idea or belief, no longer something that the 'teacher' at the front of the room who seems to have all the answers has got that we need to get, but it becomes *ours*, our own lived reality.

We *are* our experience: every sound, colour and texture, everything and everyone—black/white, rich/poor, Christian, Catholic, Jew, Muslim, gay/straight, genius/fool, every colour, every creed—the achievements and the set backs, the delight and the heartbreaks, the certainties and gnawing doubts. And yes even the very misunderstanding that we are exclusively contained inside a body of flesh and bone, along with all the defensive patterns and behaviours which that belief engenders. This is not a mistake, a universal error, but yet another expression emerging out of our endless creativity. And so too of course, in true dualistic fashion, is this message of freedom, releasing us from that inhibiting belief.

All is ourself, our primal, original nature, shape shifting into a myriad of seeming forms, characters and circumstances, a cocktail of emotion and sensation, creating this rich play of experience in all its tragicomic splendour—every scene, every entrance and every exit of this masterpiece of drama that is life.

And what wonders unfold as this understanding deepens and matures. In seeing that everyone is only ever doing their very best in the given circumstances, all is forgiven; forgiveness for a lifetime of beating oneself up for not being good enough, beautiful enough, successful enough, exciting enough, or whatever our particular hang ups might be; forgiveness for all 'others' too, who have supposedly hurt us or done us wrong. In the end even forgiveness falls apart. We are the guilty and the innocent, the attacker and the victim, the repressor and the repressed, the judger and the judged. There is no 'other' to blame or to forgive.

In recognising that we are only ever meeting ourself, closer than close, more intimate than intimate, the longing for something more dissolves, swallowed up in fathomless depths of love.

Then, "So this is it?" is transformed from a glib mental complaint into a joyous celebration, exclamation, exultation of the magical wonder of this eternal present . . .

THIS *IS* IT!

The Promised Land

When I first ventured into the world of spirituality I found myself in a group whose core teaching was all about self purification. The walls of the centre were adorned with prints of renaissance paintings, such as Saint George slaying the dragon, to inspire and motivate us students to become spiritual warriors engaged in the 'inner' struggle of 'good' versus 'evil'. And the goal of this holy war on oneself? To exterminate all the 'bad' in us and so reach the 'promised land'.

And as the holy war breaks out it's not a pretty sight. We find a whole army of evil phantoms marching in our thoughts. They tell us we're no good, a talentless waste of space, an unlovable bum. But as soon as we reach for our trusty sword of truth they change tack, persuading us that we need them desperately: to appear intelligent and exciting, to be loved and admired, that they are the ones who protect us and make us the best that we can be. This is a powerful riposte and we feel a little dazed, but it's early days and our determination is strong and we're soon leading the charge once more. A thought pops up out of nowhere, "How can it be that I am so defiled with sin?" We start to blame our parents, our teachers, our culture, blame, blame, blame argh! There's the fiend again! Then we feel guilt for all the blaming, guilt, guilt, guilt argh! And again! We reach for our sword once more but the enemy is a cunning master of disguise and suddenly switches sides, becoming all conciliatory, even offering to help draw up a list of all the offending evil thoughts in need of extermination—and would we like the list in alphabetical order? And so it goes on and on.

Thoughts attacking in packs with whole multi layered stories of how we've been wronged and abused, or how we've been negligent and irresponsible; feelings of anxiety, fear and desire all raining down with thoughts judging thoughts judging thoughts.

Exhausted and feeling utterly besieged we leave the battlefield for another day. But our supposed enemy doesn't leave us. They hide in our lazy, comfy sofa and our cup of tea, offering a little gossip over just a little extra slither of chocolate cake. They whisper in our ear as we're dozing off to sleep, and crawl into our dreams to continue their taunting and teasing!

Sooner or later we realise that this kind of inner conflict is a joyless and endless cycle of self recrimination. The cruel reality is that, no matter how devotional we are to the cause, we can never reach that longed for 'promised land', for it's the utter conviction that we are exclusively a separate someone in need of purification *that creates the very tendencies we are trying to destroy!*

So what if we turn this whole fruitless quest on its head? What if this already *is* the promised land? What if it *includes* our fear, desire, anxiety and guilt, as well as all those wayward thoughts that we try so unsuccessfully to repel?

Can we be open to these thoughts and feelings without being ashamed of them? Without trying to eliminate them as being bad, unwanted or unspiritual? Without accusing oneself of being faulty or no good? Can we see them all as simply the energy of life arising and dissolving, expressing however it expresses? And if we can't, and the cycle self recriminations kick in, *what if that's ok too?!*

In falling into the arms of our own kindness, in the unconditional embrace of all that is, there is healing for this deep cut in the body of life which seemingly separates 'me' from 'you' from the 'world'. For in that absence of conflict, that gentle easing and softening, the conceptual edges melt away and we finally taste the unity for which we truly seek—the wholeness of being.

Here is where true peace lies, for being never moves. *Here* is where true happiness lives, for being wants for nothing. *Here* is where true love flows, for being knows no bounds.

As this show of duality plays on we are never just one side of the coin, or indeed both sides, but the very metal in which both sides are pressed. And what an astonishing, unfolding mystery that show delivers—the beauty and the torment, the harmony and the discord, the celebration and the humiliation. This precarious, delicate human nature yields such depth of feeling, such raw intensity, such deep caring, and yet is gone in a flash, in an instant, impossible to hold onto, making this heart break open a thousand times over.

And here I AM, shining, fresh and alive, giving life to all—to this breath, to this thought, to this utterly indescribable moment we call 'the present'.

The Prodigal Son

Many of us are drawn into spiritual seeking not to achieve those lofty goals of 'liberation' or 'enlightenment', but out of a deep feeling of disconnection, a yearning to truly meet others beyond the superficial, to rediscover the deep love that we feel we've lost.

As we journey along 'the path' we hear the message that the separate 'me' we believe ourself to be—the supposed thinker, do-er and chooser—is simply that, a belief, a grand delusion. But the full gravity of that message has such radical implications, is so utterly devastating to our current world view, that it often remains purely conceptual and not our lived reality. However willing, however open we are to the possibility that we are much more than we imagine ourself to be, rather than risk falling into the unknown we can't help but cling to our familiar repertoire of self images—even the 'I'm useless', 'I'm guilty', 'I'm scum' beliefs seem preferable to that sense of total abandonment.

And so we hang in there, adding a few more spiritual books and videos to the pile (and certainly not a novel or a hollywood blockbuster!) wondering which sentence will deliver the magic silver bullet that will end all the yearning. We turn the next page and there it is again, "'you' are not the author of your life!" But it still *feels* as if, without the supposed 'me' in charge, our world will surely fall apart and we'll end up in some kind of terrible danger; how exactly that danger looks is uncertain, for it lurks like a terrifying monster that is always just out of sight, but we can feel its grisly presence.

We inquire and seek, seek and inquire with ever increasing intensity until the frequency may reach fever pitch. Perhaps we wish we'd never started in the first place and could call the whole thing off, but we can't! Our thoughts become a boxing match between 'me' and 'myself': 'I'm almost there', 'there is only here'; 'I've finally got it!', 'there's nothing to get'; 'argh I've lost it!', 'there's nothing to lose' . . . on and on it goes, round after round, until we finally fall to the floor with exhaustion.

In the still aftermath of our frenzied seeking, our utter failure to get 'there' becomes our blessing.

With nowhere left to look and nothing left to hold, the essence of that terrifying/relieving message finally starts to dawn. As we fall into our fears, as we expose our deep sense of vulnerability, it's not that the seeker becomes a finder but the very notion of a 'me' that seeks falls apart.

We are like the prodigal son who, having separated from his father, loses everything. Feeling empty, hungry and full of sorrow, he finally comes to his senses and returns once more to his father's land to beg for forgiveness. And in the joyous reunion that follows, 'we' are embraced by the 'father', into whose infinite arms we merge.

Our essential nature is revealed: we never were truly separated from the Father/God/Awareness/Presence/Being, we *are*

THAT within and out of which all arises and dissolves, *including* this unique character we imagined ourself to exclusively be, along with all its gifts and foibles.

We are a living paradox that thought could never understand: time within the timeless, dimensions within the dimensionless, form within the formless, individuality within the indivisible—the ultimate game of dressing up.

With every step along the journey we were already home; being each step, the journey and the traveller. Our emptiness overflows with the fullness of life—we are the wind in the trees, the splash of rain in a puddle, the movement of the breath, the beat of the heart, an opening door and a welcoming smile, a cosy room on a cold winter's day, a cup of tea and a biscuit, the taste and texture of biscuit on the tongue, the warmth of the cup in the hand. Where is the edge of that sensation? Where do I this aware presence end and that sensation begin?! Every situation, every experience, every single perception is singing out, "Hello! Here You are! This is You, You *being* this-right-now. Hello!"

As those old mis-beliefs begin to melt away, that deep, divine Love that seemed lost is rediscovered. Not love as a blissful feeling that comes and goes, not my love for you or your love for me, but Love that recognises itself in all that is—in each and every facet of this glorious, exhilarating, gut wrenching, heart breaking, vertigo inducing, roller-coaster ride of being alive.

No matter how expressive our language, however precise our choice of vocabulary, however talented we are at spilling the contents of our heart onto the page, it's never that.

Inexpressible, incomprehensible, unavoidable—" . . . "

Deep Honesty

"Why do I want to know the truth of who I really am?"

If we ask ourself that question and are deeply honest in our reply then we may be surprised at what comes up. Perhaps we imagine that we'll become special, and be admired, loved and revered by others; that we'll finally be noticed and get the recognition and attention we've always craved; or that all our problems and discomfort will instantly vanish and our life will become endlessly blissful.

It may be embarrassing to admit such imaginings but, if we are open to feeling the rawness of that humiliation, then deep honesty is our greatest tool.

We can begin to acknowledge how, in all our fantasising, we lose sight of the obvious fact that all these wonderful benefits are still for the separate 'me'; 'me' who always wants to control life—to get pleasure and escape pain; 'me' who is built out of the very sense of longing and lack that it's trying to escape.

And so the feeling of separation is only enhanced, driving more seeking, creating more separation, driving more seeking. We may go to the ends of the earth, taking on the most severe practises, whilst all the while aggrandising an ever more special, super hard core, spiritual 'me'.

If we appeal to that deep honesty once more, and sink through the layers of our seeming separate self, what do we discover?

Beneath all the seeking and longing there lurks a deeply uncomfortable feeling of restlessness, loneliness and insecurity. Dare we feel the burn of that dis-ease before rushing off into some new diversion?

Sink deeper, deeper in, and there, despite all our pretending to the contrary, we find worthlessness, inadequacy and unlovability. Dare we feel into the pain of that, without rationalising it all away?

Go deeper, deeper still. For beneath the gnawing agitation, the worthlessness and unlovability, the anger, sadness, guilt and shame, when we're utterly laid bare, what's left is the terror of being nothing at all—a deathly absence.

In fully opening to the seeming horror of that nothingness, that abyss, without turning away, without fleeing back into our world of make-believe, without expecting anything in return—no specialness, no recognition, no eternal bliss—the miraculous revelation is that we are not destroyed! On the contrary, we come to realise all that we truly long for—the indestructible love that is our essential, undivided nature.

In that glorious realisation, there is no longer anything to uphold or protect; our suit of armour is outmoded and redundant, on its way out to the mounting scrapyard of beliefs.

We become so good at pretending that we end up believing our pretence, continually upgrading to the latest version to keep up with the rest, not realising that everyone else is pretending too! And there's the laughter. We can laugh at all the multi level game playing, the convoluted story making, the deadly seriousness, the escapist fantasies and the deep misunderstandings.

The breath of Love gives life to all. Love sees its own face shining in every fallen leaf, in every star, and all that lies between.

Christmas with the Relatives

Many of us will be travelling to see relatives this Christmas perhaps with a slight sense of trepidation. Being back in the house we grew up in we may feel those old, painful patterns re-emerging, see the replaying of those same old dramas, feel ourself being related to as someone we once were and not who we now are.

We may regret that our families don't understand us, that they are still hopelessly lost in the dream and unable to meet us where we are, unable to connect on a deeper level. But when we make such judgements it is really *us* who are deluded, *us* who are lost in the dream—the dream of being spiritually 'awake', of being somehow special, better and beyond these 'lowly' kinds of interactions.

It can be a disturbing truth to face—that all our supposed spiritual superiority is actually serving to separate us further off from rather than reconnect us back to life.

It's no one else's job to understand us. However we imagine we'd like others to be is our own fantasy, that keeps us from embracing them as they are, that keeps us from the possibility of truly meeting.

So what if when we return home we are simple and open hearted? What if when our father asks which route we took and how much the petrol was per litre, and our mother asks us if we're eating properly we recognise that they are really saying, "I love you." She grew us inside her, felt us kicking in her belly, gave birth to us; they watched us growing up, poured their affection into us and then watched us walk away. That connection is unbreakable.

Without all our spiritual baggage, when we are truly honest and laid bare, only then can we really meet one another. That's when our Christmas can transform from a feeling of trepidation to a joyous celebration of love.

PART 2: 2014

The Real Story

A friend was telling me about a time when she was at school and had to produce a piece of descriptive writing for homework. She had no idea what to write about so kept on putting it off. Eventually it came to the evening before the homework was due and the piece still remained unwritten.

That night she lay restlessly awake in bed, huddled tight beneath the blankets, hugging her knees, looking into the cold, pale moon peering in at her through the curtains, wondering what ridicule and punishment she would receive the next day for her failure to complete the task. Tears seeped into the pillow and she felt increasingly anxious.

Woken by his daughter's distress, her father came into the room to see what was the matter. She told him everything and they went downstairs to work on the piece together. But despite her father's best intentions he too found the task overwhelming. They both looked down at the terrifying blank page before them demanding to be filled.

In the end, after much sweat and many more tears, they managed to scrape something passable together just to get through the whole misery unscathed. And as she described this old memory to me in vivid detail, still deeply moved by the kindness, concern and understanding her father had shown her, it struck me that *this* was the *real* story, rather than the one they had sweated to cobble together (which incidentally she could no longer recall). But she had never even thought to write about her *present* experience, assuming it to be of no value—just a boring, painful moment in need of escaping—automatically diving into thinking to come up with something 'worthy' and 'acceptable'.

This is exactly what we do in life all the time—overlook our current experience in favour of the abstract conjurations of thought. As John Lennon put it, "Life is what happens to you while you're busy making other plans."

So what do we discover when we simply STOP?

Initially it may feel like an unbearable 'blankness' compared to our usual rampant thinking and doing. There may be an incredible urge to race off into the next thought or activity. But what happens when we just stay here a while, and become a little more familiar with 'blankness'? We start to notice that, without any effort whatsoever, sounds are happening, breathing is happening, there are pulsing, tingling sensations and vibrations, smells and tastes, feelings, colours and textures—a continually shifting kaleidoscope of perceptions. That 'blankness', that 'empty nothing' is utterly full of everything, is teeming with aliveness. Without our thought frame to define, categorise and partition the experience up into 'me' and 'not me', we *are* this *entire*, edgeless slab of life.

And there are thoughts arising and dissolving too. Maybe thoughts that agree or disagree with these words, that may judge, resist or compare, that may feel angry and offended and rush to protect some idea about who we are—all passing through like leaves floating on the surface of a river.

In clearly seeing life as it *is*, in clearly seeing all the mental confusion and not needing anything to change, *change happens*; more and more of the old beliefs join the procession of flotsam and jetsam and are carried away by the current.

It's in this simple opening to life that we shift from feeling restless, anxious and afraid, to relaxing into the joyous appreciation of our natural wonder.

Smiling Buddha

Whenever we're feeling anxious, restless or dissatisfied, seeing that iconic figure of the smiling Buddha sitting in stillness can be inspirational, encouraging us to take a moment's pause . . . to breath . . . to relax . . . That experience of peace can bring such relief from the familiar contracted, clumped up, disquiet of living that we understandably want to hold on to it.

So we may try to emulate our spiritual teachers who seem to have got 'there', and go to work on cultivating and establishing a permanent 'state' of peace and happiness. Out of our dense, coagulated discomfort we carve a shrine to stillness, and there we sit in meditative concentration to shut out all the turmoil. But no matter how hard we try, our shrine walls have a habit of collapsing in, exposing us once more to all that unwanted agitation.

And so begins our personal struggle: fighting to reclaim that hallowed ground of tranquility, whilst being continually swept away by the irrepressible force of life. We may try harder and harder to stand our ground, become more and more disciplined, put in more and more effort, super-effort, until finally we grow weary of all the struggling and come to a point of absolute despair.

This hopeless moment is our greatest gift!

Why? Because we finally give up on a struggle that can never be won. For despite all our spiritual talk about not manipulating life in any way, about simply allowing it to be 'as it is', dividing our feelings up into the ones we want and the ones we don't want is the greatest manipulation of all!

And what is at the root of all this manipulation? The need to escape discomfort. And why do we need to escape discomfort? Because of the conviction that we're separate, isolated and under threat.

But it's this very conviction that gives rise to all the discomfort from which we're trying to escape!

All that unwanted agitation seems like a pack of hungry, howling wolves we've been struggling to keep from the door. And in our hopelessness, with no other way to turn, we finally dare to let down our guard. As the wolves rush in we feel the full onslaught of our self doubts and criticisms, our deepest fears and resentments, our tortuous memories and chronic resistance—feel the invasion of all that we could never bear, that we've been pushing down our whole life, all rising up demanding to be heard.

And lo and behold, right there, in the middle of this energetic maelstrom, we discover that we're still here, still alive, maybe more alive than ever before! That who we really are is like an edgeless container, within and out of which all these intense energies are arising and dissolving, that is in itself unscratchable, unscrapeable, indestructible.

To who we really are those vicious wolves are made of paper and offer us no threat. In fact they are never our enemy but only ever our dearest friends, howling their loudest to wake us from the dream of believing that we're separated off from life 'out there'.

As all that contracted, clumped up energy finally finds its long lost voice and releases into our boundlessness, so too does our need to segregate life. And in the wholeness that remains, we understand for ourself the deeper meaning of that icon of the smiling Buddha:

True peace and happiness are not 'states' we need to try to hold on to or cultivate, but the nature of what we already, effortlessly *are*.

Piranhas

My eldest son has a great t-shirt with 5 different coloured, sharp toothed piranha fish embroidered on the front. Once we were naming the colour of each fish in English and Italian (his mum is from Sicily): purple – viola, yellow – giallo, orange – arancione, blue – blu and green – verde. It was only later, as he was running across the room, that I noticed the entire t-shirt was brown! In focussing solely on the embroidery we had neglected to recognise the most obvious colour of all, that of the t-shirt itself, without which there would be no little piranhas.

Similarly in life we have come to overlook the wonder of our essential nature, becoming instead fixated solely on the content of the experience, out of which we identify ourself exclusively with one small fragment—the separate 'me'.

Just as the material of the t-shirt enables the embroidered design to exist, so what we truly are is the very fabric of all that is, giving life to those sharp toothed piranhas, the neglected t-shirt, this story, the thoughts that reflect upon it, the movement of breath, the sensation of blood coursing through the veins—the entire expression of this inexplicable, shape shifting, magical moment.

The Last Crusade

Why am I here? What is life all about? What is the purpose of existence? These are the questions that many of us find ourselves facing at some or maybe many points in our life.

We may rummage through the latest theories of science and philosophy, but whatever new concepts we take on, however ingenious, they never seem to wholly satisfy. We may delve into religion and spirituality, but despite hearing the whisper of something familiar, something beautiful, we often find them overly dogmatic and impenetrable—a new collection concepts to add to the ever growing pile. We share our questions with friends, family and colleagues, but find that the general response is not to worry about it too much, to just get on with life and make the best of it.

In finding no satisfactory solution many of us give up seeking those seemingly elusive answers and instead immerse ourself once more in the busyness of life—to drown out all the anxiety that those 'big' questions seem to provoke.

But some of us simply cannot settle for less and keep on looking. We jump from book to book, from spiritual path to spiritual path as our tireless quest continues to prove fruitless; until maybe a new question arises which, before now, had never even been considered:

Who is the one that is asking all the questions?

Are we really the separate, limited entity that our stock of second-hand knowledge would have us believe?

In our childlike, first-hand experience, can we find whatever is knowing these words? That is knowing the thought that says, "Yes, it's in my head"? That is knowing the bundle of sensations we label 'my head'? That knows the sound of birdsong as intimately as the tingling in our fingers?

In exploring our deeply held assumptions we find ourself at the edge of our thought-made version of reality, the edge of reason, facing a seeming chasm of uncertainty. We imagine that to fall into that abyss of not knowing would lead to insanity, that we'd no longer be able to function in the world, and so we retreat from the edge, back into the apparent safety and support of our familiar structures of knowledge. We may find ourself there on that ledge again and again, held back by an invisible barrier of fear, unable to move beyond.

We are like Indiana Jones in 'The Last Crusade'! Standing precariously at the edge of the abyss, "Only in the leap from the lion's head will he prove his worth," says the Holy Grail diary. "It's a leap of faith!" cries Indy in disbelief.

When the longing for the truth overshadows our fears, or we're inspired by a deep and profound sense of love, or else we suffer some personal tragedy and our known world simply crumbles to pieces, that mysterious movement takes place— we courageously step through that barrier of fear, fall from the edge of that precipice, and . . .

. . . nothing happens! We don't die, we don't go mad or experience unspeakable violence; rather, in moving beyond the constraints of our mind frame, we feel vivified and vibrantly alive.

In the film, Indy steps into the gaping chasm only to discover he is supported by an invisible bridge. He then finds the Holy Grail—a cup from which his dying father drinks and is miraculously healed of his mortal wounds.

But the 'Holy Grail' we discover is no physical object with supernatural qualities, it is true Self realisation. We see life beyond the naming and framing of thought, and find a living fabric of colours, shapes and forms, interwoven with a soundscape, a feelingscape, with tastes, smells and thoughts, with pulsing, tingling energetic aliveness, and what we truly are is knowing and being the substance of every thread of this living tapestry. It's with that recognition that our own healing can begin. Healing from the dis-ease and psychological suffering born of the mis-belief that we are but a limited fragment of life.

We don't then abandon our concepts and education; we can enjoy playing in the realm of ideas, of language, of number. We just appreciate their limitations—that who we really are could never be understood by a thought. Even the three wise men, with all their great knowledge, bow down before the baby Jesus. Unlocked from their rigid, literal interpretations, we see the deeper truth of the world's great religions.

And what of our quest for the meaning of life?

In believing the very thought that asks the question, we simultaneously create its counterpart, the belief in a separate 'me' in need of an answer. Similarly, as the belief that we are a fragment of life dissolves, so too do all the questions.

And in that sacred union we go from longing, to loving and celebrating this wondrous miracle of being.

Blown Apart

When everything around us falls apart, when the things we thought were safe and secure and never had to doubt are pulled like a rug from under our feet, when all our well laid plans are totally obliterated, we find ourself longing for some kind of security in this chaotic vortex of existence.

What a gift, what an absolute wonder to recognise right there, in the eye of the storm, the only true security there ever really is—the very fact of our being.

Whether we suffer a bereavement, the break up of a relationship, the loss of a job or the shock of a health scare, however tragic the circumstances, however intense the feelings, our being is never shaken, just as the waves crashing on the surface of a fathomless ocean cannot disturb the calmness of its depths —that silence, that stillness is imperturbable.

This is not to deny what's happening, on the contrary. In recognising our indestructibility, the pain, the fear, the sorrow and despair can all be deeply met, greeted as another unique expression of our infinite creativity.

Can there even be a newfound sense of freedom as our latest world view is blown apart?

Daring to Burn

When we first delve into the world of non-duality, it can be mind blowing to discover that we are not exclusively a limited self, contained inside a body; that who we really are is this limitless, undivided presence, knowing and being the entire expression of life. However, as that initial euphoria begins to fade, we often find we're still longing for something more, still getting anxious and frustrated, maybe even more so. To make matters worse, when we go looking for further guidance, we find so many different, often contradictory messages from writers and teachers, that it only adds to our confusion.

Some tell us that getting locked up in anxiety and frustration is a sure sign that we still believe we are separated off from life. And so, in wanting to be free of those uncomfortable feelings, we inadvertently begin judging ourself for being such a failure, and that for all our seeking we still don't get it, that we'll never get it, that everyone else gets it but us. We may then judge ourself for having judged ourself, which is only more judgment; or we resist our mental resistance, which is only more resistance; or else we deny that these feelings are even happening, wearing instead a glowing spiritual smile to hide all the inner turmoil. What a mess!

Others tell us that 'this is it', that 'everything is awareness', that all our anxiety and frustration is simply life happening. This can bring a great sigh of relief and a seeming magical end to all those brutal self recriminations. But again, as time goes on, we find ourself still longing for more, still suffering in those old familiar ways, for the deep feeling that we are separate from life remains intact, only now dressed up and masquerading in spiritual clothing, pulling out the trump card of 'everything is awareness' to win any argument—the ultimate justification for all our fear based reacting.

Our thought stream is such a slippery character that it can quickly hijack any new insight we might glean, and non-duality is not immune. We can read all the books, visit all the teachers and build a beautiful conceptual structure of what it's all about, but until we are willing to explore that murky world of our feelings, then the psychological suffering continues to torment us.

So where do we go from here?

Whenever that suffering flares up, right there, in the heat of the moment, we get curious about it, we explore it intimately, we see the mental busyness trying to resist the intensity of the feeling, trying to bandage up the rawness with stories of distraction, we see the whole mechanism of 'me' rising up, born of the fear of being overwhelmed, the fear of being destroyed, the fear of fear itself.

Can we courageously fall into that fear? Courageously feel the explosion of energy, the waves of hot/icy, dense emotion? Feel the heartbeat thumping louder and faster, the heaviness of the breath? Can we even see the exquisite beauty in that powerful energetic dance?

For when we dare to burn through all the layers, we miraculously discover that we are not destroyed, that we're not even scratched! That we have been needlessly splitting ourselves apart, needlessly creating our own mental suffering, needlessly barricading off this rich, energetic dimension of our being out of the deep delusion that we are a separate self under threat— a self that derives its very existence from all of our resistance.

Then it's our children, our partners, our families, friends and work colleagues that become our ultimate teachers; offering a continual supply of fresh opportunities to lift the lid on life and illuminate all the dark corners where the trick of 'me-ing' still operates. And as we courageously open to this pulsating world of aliveness, our painful memories that were locked up and buried deep down are finally set free; free to express, free to release, welcomed home from their banishment in an infinite, loving embrace.

As we naturally lose interest in all the mental resisting, the peace inherent in our being begins to pervade our daily experience, deepening and enriching, unlocking and enlivening our character, our relationships, our lives.

The Complete Sandwich

Whilst on a retreat, at the end of a beautiful exchange, the man I was speaking with experienced an image of a sandwich but was unsure quite what it meant.

What immediately came to mind was how we're often so focused on the content of life—the filling—that we completely overlook the bread—our boundless, essential nature—within which the 'filling' of life appears. But in living this way something seems amiss, we feel a sense of dis-ease, of incompleteness. We may try to change our life circumstances, change the flavours, but that sense of lack remains, for you simply cannot have a filling without any bread!

Then we get interested in spirituality and become so focused on discovering the 'bread' that now we neglect the filling—our fragile human nature. But in living this way we feel empty and hollow, still feeling all that yearning, still feeling that same sense of lack.

Ultimately we realise that wholeness is not exclusively the 'filling', nor exclusively the 'bread', but the complete sandwich! That's when we finally savour the full, rich flavour of living.

Just as we were all feeling rather satisfied with this grand interpretation, a mischievous snigger rose up from someone else in the group. When invited to share their amusement they replied, "I was just thinking maybe he's hungry?"

The Real Signalman

It's amazing the places that the perennial wisdom turns up. Whilst watching an episode of Thomas the tank engine with the family (written interestingly by the Reverend Wilbert Awdry) we came across this little gem:

Gordon: *(boasting to the other engines)* I've pulled expresses for years and have never once lost my way. I seem to know the right line by instinct.

Narrator: Every wise engine knows of course that the signalman sets the switches to make the engines run on the right tracks. But Gordon was so proud he had forgotten.

When we really believe we're in control of life, if things go well we can become very pleased with ourselves indeed. But how we suffer when the switches change and we run on the 'wrong' track.

But that suffering is a call back home, a call to recognise that what we really are is not exclusively a separate little engine, but life itself: the fizzling firebox, the bubbling boiler, the smell of smoke and steam, the passing countryside, the waving onlookers and the passengers waving back; a call to recognise that there is no 'wrong' track, that it's Life/Knowing/Awareness/God that is the real signalman and always was.

(Quotation from *James the Red Engine* by the Reverend Wilbert Awdry, first published in 1948)

The Cycle of Criticism

You're queuing at the supermarket checkout and the person in front is putting their shopping on the conveyer belt. Suddenly up pops a thought criticising their eating habits, drinking habits and state of health. You overhear some people chatting, up jumps another thought criticising their accent, vocabulary and conversation. You're walking home and thought is running wild, criticising the way people look, their weight, their clothes, their hair, make up, nose, ears, mouth, teeth, smile!

And what is the pay off for all this rampant criticising? A dose of superiority, a hit of self-satisfaction, and the comforting feeling that we 'know it all'.

But once we get wise to what's going on, then comes perhaps the most vehement criticism of all: the self-criticism for having been so critical! Then our seemingly cast iron smugness instantly morphs into a deep sense of embarrassment, guilt and shame.

This is the cycle that plagues many of us; we wish it wasn't so, yet nothing seems to change and we're left feeling tormented and frustrated.

But what exactly is this separate 'self' around which all our 'self' righteousness and 'self' reproach revolves?

A collection of thoughts, feelings and sensations.

But hold on, our thoughts are continually changing, and sometimes there are none at all. Our feelings are always coming and going, and the same is true of sensations—just clap your hands and the stinging in your palms immediately begins to fade; and what of the image of the body? If we simply close our eyes, is it anywhere to be found?

In our *actual* experience we find no fixed, permanent self whatsoever.

When we invest our entire identity in appearing and disappearing perceptions, we become the very definition of insecurity. That's why we judge and criticise, that's why we manipulate the truth, that's why we tell disparaging stories about others: to try to substantiate and aggrandise our imagined 'self', to try to escape the restless discomfort of feeling utterly insecure.

So what is it that sees this whole drama playing out?

This aware presence that we truly are, that never comes and goes, that is the only real security there is; that is expressing itself as everyone and everything, unchanging yet ever-changing, like clay shaping and reshaping into an endless variety of forms whilst never becoming anything other than clay. This knowing presence, that has no quarrel with the critic the criticising or the criticised, just as the paper has no preference over the story that fills its page.

Of course that doesn't mean that if we're being treated in an unreasonable or unloving way we should never complain. On the contrary! We can be absolutely direct in taking a stand, in naming what's unacceptable, since that movement comes from a natural, impartial discernment and not the need to uphold our precarious sense of self. Appreciating the difference is something for us all to continually explore.

And yes our heart will still bleed when we see cruelty to children or animals, when we see humanity's inhumanity to humanity and the environment. But in understanding that our judgements are only ever aimed at ourself, our criticism of 'others' turns into compassion, for all these actions are generated by the deep ignore-ance of our real abiding nature—our indivisible unity.

When the critical thoughts start to roll, this is not about trying to stop them, wishing them away or punishing ourself for having them (but if we do, what if that's ok too?!).

Instead they come as love's special envoys, inviting us to see the mechanism of separation at work, to see through our literal self-centredness, to see that this creation called life is woven together with strands of love, unravelling and refashioning in ever changing patterns and forms, that every experience, every conversation, every character—in all their colours, shapes and sizes, with all their quirks and eccentricities—are really our essential nature shining in a multitude of ingenious disguises, inviting us to delight once more in the glorious majesty of being.

The Cosmic X-Ray

What happens when we feel like a talentless waste of space, a no hoper, a useless failure? Maybe we like to develop the theme further with stories about our worthlessness, our self-delusion—that we're ineffective, unproductive, that everyone else is so much more talented than we are; or else we seek out excuses and justifications—if only we had more time, if only we had more money, if our job were different, if the kids were older, if we lived in a different country, in a different time in history, if if if . . .

But there is another possibility, the path less travelled: to go beyond the realm of thought and its stories, and come directly into the rawness of the moment—the visceral world of sensation, of aliveness; to feel the high voltage of our anxiety and frustration—its tense, edgy, nervy, restlessness—to welcome it, to honour it in all its intensity; for the hard shell of the in-sufficient 'me' to split wide open and be immersed in the fear of uncertainty, of vulnerability, of being utterly laid bare; to abandon oneself completely to the exhilarating aliveness of it all.

It's then that the great synthesis can unfold and, like a shaft of sunlight pouring through a gap in the clouds, the joy of being floods in, penetrating life with its wavelengths of truth.

And what does this cosmic X-ray reveal? Everything is made of atoms of love! Jiggling and vibrating away in their merry dance of sweet perfection.

Dear Parents Everywhere, I Salute You!

It's 1 am and the kids are screaming. Maybe it's teething again, or the fear of the dark; maybe a bad dream, or simply over excitement. But whatever it is, this is another night of broken sleep to add to the weeks, months, years of mounting sleep deprivation. And then there's the incessant cooking, cleaning, washing, feeding, soothing, supporting, entertaining, distracting, boundary setting, boundary enforcing . . .

As you stand there, calming and rocking, you feel like you want to cry. But beneath those tears is a smile as wide as the universe, for the inconceivable joy, the fathomless depths of feeling, the heart bursting love that these wondrous little beings inspire; for being taught the true meaning of patience, of sacrifice, of devotion; for appreciating how every challenging moment of this rich dimension of the human experience is a magical gift, wrought in the fires of love.

It's 3:30 am and all is calm . . . for now. As your little gurus lie tucked up in their beds, dear parents everywhere, I salute you!

"Calm Down"

A loved one is frustrated, angry, maybe fuming with rage. We see their distress and try to 'help' the situation by imploring them to "calm down", but instead of making things better it only makes them worse! So what's really going on beneath those seemingly innocent two words?

The uncomfortable truth is that *we* literally can't bear the anxiety their distress is causing *us*. That's why we want them to 'calm down', 'cheer up' or 'try and forget about it'—to be rid of our own agitation so we can feel at ease. And in trying to change their behaviour we make them wrong; wrong for being angry, sad or worried, and so add guilt, blame and shame to their mounting pile of suffering. Maybe we even get angry back, or else become distant and unreachable, withdrawing our love as punishment for their actions. This is the chain of reactivity that destroys relationships, wrecks marriages and ruins lives.

Now ask yourself this: does anyone really choose to be angry, sad or worried? Does anyone get out of bed in the morning and decide to mess up their life and the lives of everyone they love?

When we behave in this way we're caught in the powerful grip of thousands of years of human conditioning; conditioning that's built around one fundamental belief: that what we are is a separate fragment of life, exposed and under threat. As soon as we take on that belief we start the chain that, like falling dominos, leaves us no choice but to continually react—continually trying to escape pain and find some kind of security.

What if, when we see another in distress, we can recognise that they're swept up in the momentum of an ancient, deeply ingrained habit, that's not of their choosing, that they're not even aware of? That our own urge to react, as well as whatever guilt or shame we might feel for having that urge, is also part of that very same momentum? Then, instead of blaming or judging, we find we're naturally filled with compassion and forgiveness—for oneself as well as for the other.

Then, maybe we can truly meet them in their anguish, their torment, feeling our own anxiety and frustration without needing to attack, escape, deny or disconnect, without needing to suppress them or ourself.

Maybe we can come together right there—in the raw, tender, burning heat of the human condition—where the walls of separation melt away to reveal not annihilation, not unimaginable pain, but inconceivable, immeasurable love, and a peace beyond all understanding.

Doing the Dishes

You're doing the dishes, locked inside a torrent of thinking. Suddenly you notice the warmth of the water on your hands, the tightness in your stomach and shoulders, the shortness of your breath. And in that simple, innocent noticing, slowly, as if by magic, the scene begins to open, the tension naturally begins to soften, the breath begins to deepen; you hear the rustling of the wind in the trees outside, the distant sound of traffic, the whole bustling soundtrack of life.

And whatever you are that is noticing—that notices the throbbing pulse of the heart equally as the sound of children playing, the bubbles of foam on the water as intimately as the tingling sensation of the face—is undoubtedly here, but nowhere to be found; and in being unfindable, is inseparable from everyone and everything! With that realisation love wells up in your heart, spilling over, drenching every particle of this wondrous arising with its sweet nectar.

Wherever you are, whatever you're doing, whatever you're feeling, the awe of being is already here, already available, waiting patiently to be dis-covered.

Innocent Eyes

What a magical gift young children are! You're off for a walk with your little companion when suddenly you feel their tiny hand hold you back; you've been stopped mid-pavement, and with all your adult sophistication you wonder why? There's nothing to see here.

But oh how wrong you are, for in your discarded 'nothing' your little friend lends you their innocent eyes to reveal an infinite world of delight: a stream of ants teeming from a crack in the paving stone, a tiny rug of soft green moss, an explosion of grass reaching for the light, the spiral of an empty snail shell, a decaying leaf with its intricate network of veins, an assortment of minute bugs roaming the scene.

As you stare transfixed with wonder at this micro universe at play, suddenly you feel a gentle tug on your hand again. Obviously it's time to move on to some other scene of awe. You obey your new master gladly and feel the excitement, the exhilaration of having no clue about what could possibly happen next!

Life Purpose

Many of us are plagued by the pressure to find our 'life purpose'. Maybe we've tried different careers, hobbies, interests but none of them seemed to be 'the one'; or maybe we've been waiting for some flash of inspiration, some sudden revelation of what it is we're 'supposed' to be doing, but nothing has come and we're left feeling frustrated and unfulfilled.

Instead of looking for our life purpose in some job description or other, what if we look in a very different direction, and explore that very feeling of frustration and unfulfillment itself—that edgy, nervy agitation; that tense, restless unease—and simply wonder: what is it that we are that is aware of these feelings, that shines unchanging whilst the world performs its colourful dance, that remains unparted from every feature of that wondrous display?

When we look from that 'placeless place', then every vibration of sound, every tingle of sensation, every beat of the heart is already our life purpose effortlessly playing out.

In moving beyond the projections of thought, in being released from the continual self-judgements, criticisms and recriminations, and recognising the sheer miracle of what we already are, the uniqueness of our character is free to truly shine, and we're drawn very naturally to wherever we find our joy.

Black Mood

It's one of those dark days: you're plunged into a black mood, drowning in a flood of thoughts about how worthless and broken you are, about how pointless and meaningless life is. Maybe you reach for the usual techniques of trying to accept it, trying to embrace it, or else you set to work on finding the reasons why, in order to try to mend the 'problem'. Sadly all these efforts keep you stuck in that mental realm and nothing seems to shift.

Stay close to the sensual world, make the heat of the body your home, the movement of the chest, the sound of the breath, no mental reflecting is required; smell the air, see everyday people going about their business—a family in a restaurant along with Grandma and Grandpa, children playing in the park, a field of grass waving in the wind, the sound of birds, all conspiring to break you out of your thought made prison, to bring you back to simplicity.

And as those prison walls collapse away you get more than you could ever have bargained for: the unity of being is revealed and your heart cracks open with love!

Even your deepest darkness is an invitation back to the light.

Jigsaw Puzzle

You're helping a little one with a jigsaw puzzle and they seem stuck—they just can't fit that troublesome piece. But before allowing them time to figure it out, before offering words of gentle guidance, you just can't resist the powerful urge to jump in and fix it for them! For that moment of stuckness, of not-knowing, feels deeply uncomfortable, like an unbearable break in the flow of life and in desperate need of putting 'right'.

Why do we fear uncertainty? Because it leaves us with no frame of reference, no structure to cling to, and our separate sense of self feels dangerously exposed and vulnerable.

But what if there's wonder in not-knowing, a fascinating mystery to explore, a great adventure to embark on, a chance to find hidden treasure?! When we give 'the answer' we defraud our little friends of that exhilarating journey of discovery, exchanging it instead for a dull, hollow conclusion, empty of any real understanding. And so gradually we teach them to fear uncertainty as we do, and thus teach them to passively absorb the conclusions of others, of the perceived 'authority', and so live a second-hand life rather than strive for first-hand knowing.

Having grown up this way ourself, is it any wonder that when we get into spirituality we often do the same? We look to the teacher, the authority, for all the answers. We take on the new information, learn it, and wait for some kind of transformation, but nothing happens and we feel more and more frustrated.

But what if the 'teacher' is simply there to give us time, to gently guide us when we're feeling 'stuck', to facilitate and encourage us on our own magical journey of discovery?

When we reconnect with our first-hand experience, free from the dull, hollowness of second-hand conclusions, we rediscover that childlike wonder, that natural curiosity, that boundless enthusiasm; we can delight again in the excitement of not-knowing, and keep that sense of wonder alive in our children.

And in the great adventure that unfolds, we come to an astonishing realisation: the 'X' that marks the treasure spot is right where we already are.

Telling the Truth

You've lied. Maybe it's a small one or maybe a huge one, it's really all the same. Why? To maintain your precious self-image, to avoid being blamed, to avoid feeling pain. But your partner or friend is a sensitive one and, smelling the rotting odour of your lie, challenges you directly. You vigorously deny it, for to come clean is for your protective walls to be breached, your fragile core to be laid bare, the horrifying sense of your own nothingness to be shockingly exposed.

The result? Your pretence breeds distrust, breeds bitterness and discontent, and without the nourishment of truth, relationships become withered and lifeless.

But what if you dare to expose your lie and courageously feel the heat of humiliation as your painstakingly erected defence system comes crashing to the ground? What if you finally fall right into that terrifying void of your very own absence?

Freed from the burden of having to pretend, of having anything at all to uphold, you don't stop breathing, you don't die a painful death, you come wildly, ecstatically alive!

And in that delicious openness, love flows in every direction.

Flip-Flop

Have you tasted your true, boundless nature, but frustratingly find yourself feeling separate and isolated again, wondering when this 'flip-flop' will ever end?

Instead of idly waiting for some magic moment of 'grace' to call, make truth your beloved, worship it, become entirely devoted. Whenever you feel the tense, nervy agitation of resistance rising up, stay open to the discomfort, appreciate it for what it is—the separate 'me' fighting for survival. And if you close down, you close down; if you react, you react; if you judge yourself, you judge yourself. *What if that's ok?* Offer yourself that same loving kindness you gift to others, rather than reinforce the old delusion with all that 'self'-flagellation for getting it 'wrong'.

Then life becomes an adventure, every moment offering a potential enlightening revelation, even your heartache, even your misery—how exciting!

And as the mechanism of 'me-ing' is laid bare, a new confidence begins to grow: that what you truly are is never ever under threat. In being released from the preoccupation of having to avoid fear, your human character can finally celebrate its uniqueness, fully express, follow its joy; then freedom is no longer an occasional visitor, but your living, breathing reality.

Comparisons

What happens when we compare ourselves with others? Most often we feel inferior, inadequate, 'self'-critical, or else superior, puffed up and 'self'-satisfied, which is of course only inadequacy in disguise. The result? The apparent separate 'me' around which all these feelings revolve is enhanced; and consequently so too is the sense of lack, the longing for more, and the fear of losing what we already have.

Imagine every human character as being like a musical instrument, each with their own uniquely crafted shape and size, their own distinctive qualities and sound, all playing together. On becoming fixated with our own 'instrument', we immediately start comparing ourselves with others—like a flute that, on hearing the deep resonant sound a cello, imagines its own soft, floaty tones to be unworthy and so longs to become more cello-like, neglecting to recognise its own unique qualities.

But as that fixation begins to ease, we start to appreciate the full, rich texture of the music itself; we start to realise that, in our actual experience, whatever we are that is appreciating is utterly inseparable from every element of the sound, is in fact *being* this entire symphony of life.

In recognising our true indivisibility there's no longer any need for comparisons and, paradoxically, we're set free to celebrate our individuality, to fall in love with all our quirky humanness, and to finally delight in our own sweet song.

Double Bind

Do you feel bound, longing for freedom? Do you feel doubly bound, having denied your natural instinct to seek a solution because of the spiritual belief that 'there's nothing to do' because 'there's no one to do it'?

Imagine you are a small child, and you're convinced that 2 + 2 = 5. One day you're sitting with a friendly school teacher and you ask them about it. They invite you to see how 2 is made up of 1 + 1, so 2 + 2 is actually 1 + 1 + 1 + 1. You count the ones diligently and discover, for yourself, that 2 + 2 = 4 and your misunderstanding is resolved. That's life being a child with a misunderstanding. That's life being a school teacher facilitating the resolution of that misunderstanding.

Similarly life is being the message of freedom; inviting you to explore all of your assumptions, all your preconceived ideas about who you are and what life is; inviting you to feel into the fear, feel into the vulnerability, as you let go of all frames of reference, and see what remains when life-as-you-think-you-know-it falls apart.

Don't just take on more beliefs, however 'spiritual' they might seem. Look for yourself, discover first-hand. Then seeking will come to a natural end, not because you decide to do 'doing nothing' (which is the greatest doing of all!), but because you truly realise, for yourself, that you already are what you seek.

Origami

I have a friend who is really good at the Japanese art of paper folding. Whenever we're together I'll often discover a discarded scrap of paper that's been miraculously transformed into a beautiful flower.

Imagine a boundless sheet of paper, imbued with the talents of the ultimate origami master, unfolding and refolding with endless creativity into an infinite variety of forms, whilst never becoming anything other than itself.

In believing we are separate and limited we identify exclusively with one of those forms—a figure called 'me', along with 'my thoughts', 'my feelings' and 'my sensations'—that looks out at another creation called 'world', populated by lots of other separate 'mes'. Immediately we feel alienated, exposed and vulnerable, and so we try to bolster our fragile identity with self-concepts based on how we look, our abilities, our intelligence; we attach ourself to other creations such as 'my job', 'my money', 'my possessions', 'my partner', 'my children', all in a bid to find security and a sense completeness, but as this little empire of 'me' expands, that longed for security never comes. We might reach for a better job, for more money, a new partner but still that sense of completeness remains ever elusive. Stress and anxiety begin to appear as now we start to fear losing all that we've so painstakingly put together.

Then maybe we stumble upon this simple reminder: who we really are is the boundless paper out of which 'me' and everything else is made.

It sounds so very familiar, yet too troubling to truly take in as our limited sense of self feels threatened again, fearing the unknown, terrified of letting go.

But in that subtle shift in perception is anything actually lost, other than the belief that we're separate and limited? In fact in one sense nothing changes, life appears just as it always has; but in another sense everything changes. Does the paper feel alienated, exposed and under threat? Does it need to reach for anything to try to find security, to feel complete? Does it need to protect itself in any way whatsoever? In recognising our true invulnerability, our 'me' character is no longer constrained by needing to escape fear and discomfort, is finally set free to fully express, to gravitate towards its own unique calling and to truly come alive.

And what of that ultimate fear of death? The paper is never threatened by the unfolding of one of its infinitely many creations; there's rest there, like the pause at the end of an out breath . . .

. . . and after the expiration comes the inspiration, conjuring up a new, ingenious pattern of folds, giving life to a fresh, magical form—life and death, appearance and disappearance, both present in equal measure, both movements in our deepest, immutable nature.

Knowing oneself as the changeless, ever present paper is called Peace. Recognising oneself as each and every creation is called Love.

'To Do' Lists

We all have our 'to do' lists: chores to finish, projects to complete, people to see, places to go, to read more, to exercise more, to eat more healthily, to become more 'realised' or whatever it might be. But why is it that they often provoke such agitation, such impatience, such aggravating tightness?

Because we have come to believe that our happiness is dependent on completing our list of tasks, and so we yearn to reach that longed for goal. But this anxiety, this tension is so uncomfortable that we use more thought to escape it; thoughts which reaffirm that our happiness lies at the end of the list, which only increases the agitation which increases the yearning which increases the agitation which increases the yearning . . .

Before being caught up in the next cycle of thinking, what if we go deeply into that murky world of unwanted feelings— that antsy, edgy irritation?

As we open to those dancing energies, as the mental labels dissolve away, 'discomfort' is magically revealed to be none other than the pulsing, vibrating electricity of aliveness; and in vacating the confinements of thought, we find no boundaries to speak of, no reasons to escape and nothing at all to achieve.

As the longing and grasping naturally relax, joy infuses the scene, and suddenly it's clear: the happiness we seek is not dependent on any attainment, but is already always here, is the very essence of our being.

And so the play of life goes on, along with all its 'to do' lists, but rather than our actions coming from the need to escape discomfort, they can flow as an expression, a celebration, of the joy that we already are.

The Fool

"The fool doth think he is wise, but the wise man knows himself to be a fool." William Shakespeare, *As You Like It: Act 5, Sc 1.*

Why is it that Chinese Emperors, Egyptian Pharaohs and English Kings and Queens all reputedly consulted with fools and court jesters? Because the fool is unburdened by the expectations and conventions of society, is unconstrained by all the shoulds and shouldn'ts and the need to keep up appearances, is entirely free to cut through our man-made-up concepts and beliefs and to expose the unmodified truth at the heart.

So what if *we* are the fool? What if *we* dare to step outside our mental framework of ideas and explore the immediate sensual reality of the moment?

Through the eyes of the fool we discover that we have no eyes! That what we are is not an isolated person looking out at the world, but rather this entire colourful experience of life happening; that a computer keyboard is no less ourself than the fingers that dance across its keys; that the cry of a bird, the image of open sky, the sound of children playing, the taste of peppermint tea, the fizzing aliveness of sensations, the wonder of unbridled joy, the intense sorrow of grief, *every experience experienceable* is our infinitely creative being shapeshifting into ever fresh, ingenious compositions.

It's in this fool's wisdom, which our thought-made version of reality regards as pure madness, that we discover the magical homecoming for which we've always longed.

Hidden Agendas

"Welcome it. Open to it. Embrace it. Love it. Honour it. Accept it as it is." These are the words of guidance we're often used to hearing when we find ourself immersed in difficult, upsetting or emotionally painful moments in life. But when we try to follow that guidance, and the pain doesn't go away, we can become increasingly frustrated.

It's that frustration which reveals our hidden agenda—we are actually only 'honouring' and 'welcoming' the pain *in order to get rid of it*. Beneath our spiritual disguise it's the same old separate 'me' hard at work, still resisting, still trying to manipulate life, still wanting things to be different.

What if the pain were welcome to stay forever?

Then our clever thought strategy is totally obliterated. Maybe then we can hear those words of acceptance afresh, as an invitation to see life from a radically new perspective. Since our essential nature is being all that is, if something exists at all then it is *already* welcome, *already* embraced, *already* loved, honoured and accepted; and that *includes* those moments when we're caught up in the game of 'me-ing', when the pain is so great that we simply can't accept it, when we fundamentally resist, when we judge ourself for having resisted.

True acceptance is not a strategy; it has no time limit or conditions attached; it is the very essence of our being.

This is not about chastising ourself for getting it 'wrong'. That's only more of the same old game. Rather it's seeing deeply into the mechanism of how we operate, of how we're easily caught up in that old familiar model of belief, of how, when life is allowed to be truly 'as it is', then in that natural resting our suffering *does indeed* begin to unravel, and the innate joy of being shines through.

Beyond 'Mindfulness'

Performance coaches, therapists and fitness experts are doing it; nutritionists are doing it and sharing it with their clients; it's being taught in hospitals, prisons, businesses and even finding its way into the school timetable. What is the 'it' I'm talking about? The ancient practice of 'mindfulness'; of being 'present'.

Many of us who've never even opened a spiritual book or sat on a meditation cushion are now learning to simply stop . . . to observe the rise and fall of our breathing . . . and become aware of whatever thoughts, feelings, sensations, images, sounds, tastes and smells are happening in the here and now.

And what do we discover? Whether it's sadness, anxiety, frustration or total ecstasy; whether it's thoughts idly chattering away constructing a new 'to do' list, or keeping themselves busy judging and criticising oneself or others—then judging the judging, criticising the criticising and spiralling off into frantic story-making—whether it's harsh or gentle sounds, bitter or sweet flavours, pungent or fragrant smells, we start to notice that this entire kaleidoscope of experiencing is in a continual state of flux, always shifting and changing, whilst we who bear witness to it all never shift, never change, but remain constant throughout.

It's in that recognition that a newfound sense of stillness and stability may gradually begin to emerge—which many find helpful for dealing with stress, depression and addictive behaviour; for boosting attention and concentration; for finding more clarity, creativity and focus in life.

But what if we we're willing to take it one tiny step further?! What if we were to wonder: what is the nature of this 'me' that is aware of all these coming and going experiences, that in itself never changes?

Curiously the bundle of thoughts, feelings and sensations that we normally imagine ourself to be *is also part of the coming and going experience.* When we look first-hand, freshly like a child—before we reach into our previously held beliefs and assumptions—we cannot possibly define or even locate what it is that we really are. And in not being able to find ourself— where we end or even begin—can we really be separate from any of these coming and going experiences?

Our uninterpreted reality is continually proclaiming that our real, essential nature is like the ultimate shapeshifter, contorting into dimensions of space and time, into ever fresh configurations of colour, sound, sensation, smell, taste, thought and feeling, into a 'you' and a 'me', the image of these words and whatever thoughts which reflect upon them.

In that extraordinary revelation we fall in love again and again as we're wedded to every particle of life, as we recognise that this ordinary, everyday moment is an absolute miracle in action; that our partners, friends, colleagues and clients are all, in the deepest sense, expressions of our own true nature; that we can finally fully meet each 'other', even in the wildest depths of despair, and so understand the real meaning of compassion.

Then mindfulness is transformed from a useful technique for finding stillness and clarity, into a profound invitation to know oneself in a radically new way: not as a separate and isolated self, but as the source and substance of all that is.

What is Happiness?

Ask anyone what they want most out of life. What do they reply? Initially maybe 'lots of money', 'a nice house', 'a wonderful relationship'. But what if they go deeper? Why lots of money? Why a nice house? Why a wonderful relationship?

Because they think it will make them happy.

Happiness is what we truly want. When we feel un-happy, un-comfortable, we want it to go away, that's why we seek. But rather confusingly, as we embark on our seeking, we unexpectedly find ourselves encouraged to *welcome* 'un-happiness', to get *curious* about 'misery', even to grant it an open invitation to stay for as long as it likes!

What is going on we might wonder?

If we actually explore our 'bad' mood, rather than suppressing it or acting it out, what do we find? Maybe a feeling of impatience, frustration, irritation, of rising heat and tension, an acceleration of the heart beat, a tightness of the breath; maybe thoughts about how badly we're being treated, with stories of other times we've been treated this way, and the urge to fly off into a rage; or maybe a heaviness, a rawness, a sickly feeling in the stomach, and thoughts about how we want it all to magically disappear.

But how is it that we're able to report all of this?

Because what we truly are is there throughout, experiencing these 'unwanted', 'uncomfortable' thoughts and feelings like objects, arising and dissolving; and in their dissolution, we are all that is left. And what name do we give to that which remains?

Happiness.

The source of our confusion is revealed: happiness is not a good mood we need to cultivate or attain, not a state which comes and goes, but the very essence of being, within and out of which everything comes and goes.

Feedback Loop

Anyone who has ever used a PA system will know that if the microphone picks up sound from the speakers a feedback loop is created—the sound gets continually re-amplified and you hear a painful, ear splitting squeal.

Our mental suffering operates in much the same way. Whenever we find ourselves thinking anxious thoughts, our feelings begin to jangle; more thoughts then rise up to escape the bodily distress, which often only serve to raise our anxiety levels higher; then come more thoughts to escape the added discomfort, bringing more anxiety, bringing more thoughts, and on and on it goes until we're completely overwhelmed.

So where do we go from here?

Feel the two feet on the ground, bum on the seat, those three points acting like a solid mountain of support—creating a sense of rootedness, of groundedness; notice the breath, in through the nose . . . out through the mouth . . . breathing deep into the belly; loosen the jaw, the neck, the shoulders, the wrists, disengaging from the fight-flight-freeze response.

And it's from there, instead of running away into the next thought, that we courageously connect with the bodily discomfort, feel its edgy rawness, and begin to discover the revelation that, actually, it's ok, that there is no need to escape into thinking.

Slowly we become more and more confident in being the aware openness that allows *all* of life's energies to express; we begin to understand that this whole play is appearing and disappearing in our true, limitless nature, that could never be overwhelmed.

That shift in perception is like moving the microphone away from the speakers—the loop is broken, the shrill screech naturally subsides, and our unique voice rings out as a clear reflection of its source.

The Visceral Throb

When we're fed up with all our painful, unwanted conditioning, when we want our life to fundamentally change, we can
tie ourselves up in knots trying to make it happen, trying to
reach some longed for idea of 'freedom'.

"Why should it be so difficult?" we might ask.

Because the supposed 'me' that's trying to solve the 'problem'
is the cause of the 'problem' it's trying to solve! No wonder we
feel overwhelmed.

What if we just drop it all?

All the strategies, the reasoning, the spiritual concepts, the
idea of destroying our conditioning, the hope of some kind of
miracle resolution, of a permanent level of 'higher function-
ing', of becoming some super enlightened being—all of it—
and fall into total and utter abandonment, with nothing left
to hold, not even the remotest idea about what anything really
is.

Can we simply stop and be here with nothing?

Beyond all our motivations and definitions, beyond the labels
'you', 'me', 'this' and 'that' we find the visceral throb of life:
colours and forms dancing in never-to-be-repeated steps, an
impossibly elaborate symphony of sounds, the whole experience saturated in sensuality. And what if we even let go of

those descriptions? There is a happening happening. There is THIS. And through fresh, childlike eyes—without the divisions of belief—whatever is aware of THIS is utterly inseparable from it. THIS is our true body.

Life is turned inside out: what we really are is not an isolated unit, exposed and under threat, but the edgeless fabric in and out of which this whole play of experiencing is made.

With that realisation the labels and definitions are all welcome; their seeming divisions no longer disguise our wholeness. They are simply more characters in the play. Illumined by the light of understanding we see the whole mechanism of 'me' play out: the 'unwanted' conditioning rising up, the fear, the terror, the feeling of overwhelm, along with whatever thoughts flood in to the 'rescue', that try to numb and distract us from the rawness, that wrestle for control, that fight to keep us from 'danger'.

And in that unconditional openness, rather than warring with ourself, there's compassion; compassion for this antiquated mechanism that's still rattling away, still trying to save our life, still running on the old misbelief that we are but a limited self under threat.

PART 3: 2015

Who is with You Now?

Worn down, hopeless and dejected—who is with you now?

Who held you when you were told that you were stupid,
when you first learned that you were faulty goods?

Who has held you through the years
of feeling inhibited and repressed,
of yearning for more,
of pretending in order to cover all of the embarrassing awkwardness?

Who holds you when your armour of certainties turn to dust,
when you're exposed once more,
naked and raw,
with nowhere left to stand?

This One, that's who: the unnamable, the unlocatable, the
undeniable.

This One: who holds all of life in its infinite embrace.

This One: that is being these words and the reading,
this breath and the breathing,
this heart and the beating—

and it's not blood in the veins. It's love.

Beyond the Skin

A friend who once belonged to a particular spiritual group was telling me how some of the members, when feeling unhappy, frustrated or disillusioned, deliberately wouldn't attend for fear of being judged as having 'failed'.

Since when did spirituality become about denying our experience in order to uphold the image of a smiley, happy, untouchable, unflappable, super-positive, spiritual know-it-all?! Isn't it precisely the longing to be free of this kind of self-repression that draws us into 'spirituality' in the first place?

We can change the scenery, the characters and the costumes as much as we like, but until we fundamentally examine who it is we really are then that same old familiar script—of carving life up into what we should and shouldn't be feeling, denying and resisting the 'bad' whilst trying to cling onto the 'good'—will continue to play out.

So what if we look right now, in this the only moment that we ever truly have?

Whatever you are that is aware of these words is not bounded by a suit of skin, rather the image and sensation of skin arise in and out of You: You this awake spaciousness, this unlocatable, alive presence, this undeniable *am*-ness—that draws no dividing lines, that supports and sustains *everything* in experience, just as a mirror gives existence to the image of *every* reflection.

You are immense. You give life to life. You are an infinity of possibility!

There is truly nothing to fear, because there is no-thing here to protect, and nothing outside of You to be a threat. Our well fortified defence system has been operating under false intelligence!

With that realisation, instead of contorting oneself to try to 'fit in', instead of settling for the conclusions of others, we begin to trust, to revel in our own dear and precious uniqueness; to courageously meet those repressed, 'unwanted' visitors such as 'fear', 'anxiety', 'misery', 'regret'; to get to know them more intimately, beneath their sinister cloak of stories, in-the-raw, closer than close, and discover them to be nothing other than the energetic dance of aliveness.

What seemed like a prison is a playground once more, in which to explore, to discover, to follow our joy, our fascination, to celebrate and savour this mind-blowing, heart-flowing, wild roller coaster ride of being alive.

The Escape Artist

Here it comes again, that old familiar scene: tiredness, worry, anxiety, feeling lost, lonely and confused, not knowing which way to turn or what to do, feeling pressure from all sides— blocked up, closed down, hemmed in—tension in the shoulders, tension in the brow, a shortness of breath, a tightness in the belly . . .

To avoid the discomfort we reach into our usual repertoire of escape techniques: maybe it's thoughts about how faulty or deficient we are, about how we can never get our act together, about how our life is *supposed* to look; or perhaps it's a drink, or other substance of choice, or the tv remote, the credit card, or even those seemingly innocent daydreams; or maybe it's thoughts of how if only we were more awakened, more enlightened, *then* our life would open up, *then* our creativity would blossom, *then* we'd really be living 'in the flow'.

What if this 'uncomfortable' moment *already is* the very 'flow' we seek?

Instead of attempting to escape the dis-ease—which only ever brings temporary relief—what if we courageously meet those naked sensations, stripped of their mental clothing, and feel the raw, uncategorised agitation, the gnawing ache, abandon all agendas, all expectations, all manipulation and just let go, let go, let go?

In that release, as the moment opens deep and wide, what do we dis-cover?

We discover the wondrous beauty of our vastness, within and out of which each and every experience emerges and dissolves, that can never ever be destroyed, not even scratched—our original, undivided 'well' being.

In no longer trying to escape, we pull off the greatest escape of all: the escape from ever needing to escape!

We are always already free. There never are any real shackles or chains. We are free to expand beyond the limits of our comfortable numbness, to live fearlessly, to love openheartedly; free to honour and treasure our dear tenderness, our deep sensitivity; free to cherish the heartaching beauty of our precious human vulnerability.

Molten Lava

When our deepest beliefs, the ones we thought were rock solid and sacrosanct, are fundamentally shaken and crumble to dust, when our heart erupts and a molten lava flow of feelings begin to burn, how astonishing, that in the midst of these fiery energies—in no longer finding interest in the stories of fear, anger, hate or blame that try to take hold—there is nothing but gratitude and wonder for the immutable joy that is our very essence!

What is this crazy madness?! How can there possibly be joy in such 'pain'?!

Because of the felt realisation that, even in these wild extremes, our being is never diminished, charred or even touched; that truly we lack nothing, need nothing; that what we deeply are is always already utterly complete.

We are like an invisible painter, and on our palette we lay and mix not only colours, but sounds, sensations, thoughts, feelings, smells and tastes too, painting this ever-fresh, living composition called 'now'. And we don't just witness our magical creation. We are the very canvas too, holding each appearance in an inseparable embrace, in THIS the ultimate work of love.

The Greatest Show On Earthlessness

Imagine an actor who has forgotten they are acting, who believes that they literally *are* their character and that the circumstances of the play are real. Every challenging scene, every uncomfortable mixture of thoughts, feelings and sensations now feels deeply threatening and in drastic need of escaping, giving rise to all kinds of mental suffering. Then suddenly they remember their real identity again—they are the actor! They are entirely free from the limitations of the play and always were. They could never be defined or threatened by any of its make-believe characters or scenes.

So too, when we identify exclusively with the thoughts and feelings of a seemingly separate character called 'me', we psychologically suffer. Realising our true identity—the wonder of undivided being, that could never be added to or taken away from—is called happiness.

This is not to deny or devalue the 'play', regarding it as 'just a story' or some meaningless illusion. Not at all! Rather we are finally set free to *revel* in our role, to *fully* experience the intensity of those feelings and sensations without needing to escape (and even if forgetting or escaping happens that's part of it too!), free to honour every nuance of the unfolding experience, to celebrate it for the astonishing marvel it truly is.

For our essential nature is the ultimate actor, playing not just one but *every* part, in not just one but *every* story. And so too are we the costumes, the props, the scenery, the stage, the lighting, the audience, the entire production of this eternal improvisation—the greatest show on earthlessness.

Sacred Digestion

Don't run from your suffering,
don't try to interpret it,
or come to conclusions about it.

Hold it close,
meet it directly,
feel the beauty of its wild intensity.

Savour the flavour and eat it up.
Yes eat it up!
It's food for awakening.

For in that sacred digestion,
all breaks down to Love.

Game of Seduction

It's a sweet moment of clarity: the needing, grasping and clenching all fall away to reveal a wondrous, heartwarming sense of unity, of openness and ease.

Then gradually we're seduced again by our habitual, well-honed thought routines. Maybe it's relentless self evaluation, comparisons with others or old stories of resentment and injustice; maybe it's 'profound' thoughts that try to work it all out, or even a kind of 'spiritual smugness' in believing we've attained some 'higher level' of being.

And when we realise we've been fooled again, what happens then? We're down on ourself; there's frustration, irritation, that despite all our efforts nothing ever seems to change. "Why should it be so complicated?' we might wonder, and wish the struggling would vanish forever; but of course that's only more seductive thought, and so the game goes on and on. Aaargh!!!

Pause ...

Let's explore the mechanism in operation here.

In believing we're exclusively a fragile, limited 'me' we construct an armoury of self images to protect us. Whether these self images are 'positive' or 'negative' makes no difference, as long as they serve to relieve our sense of insecurity. Thought then busies itself upholding and maintaining this structure of beliefs for, so the story goes, if they are challenged or fall apart completely then the vulnerable 'me' will be dangerously exposed, and that means pain or death.

But this whole mechanism is based entirely on a deep delusion!

We're *not* a limited fraction of life, we're Infinite Being! Untouchable, unscratchable, with nothing to uphold or maintain.

In seeing clearly how the mechanism of 'me' operates, in becoming familiar with our own particular repertoire of thought routines, now whenever those 'unwelcome' thoughts come they can be honoured, yes honoured! For in their well meaning, yet misguided attempts to save the supposed separate 'me', they are actually reminding us of exactly what we're *not*.

Then ironically they *are* our saviours, for instead of confirming our separateness, they deliver us home to Love.

Enjoying the Party

A friend was telling me how she recently arrived at a party and didn't know anyone there. Immediately she felt awkward, not good enough, 'out of her power'. Sad and ashamed that as a grown woman she was still prone to feeling this way, and fearful that others might notice her awkwardness, she began forcing her behaviour—to try to make things different, to be rid of the discomfort, to not be 'found out'.

Then came an extraordinary thought: "Maybe it's ok to feel awkward?!"

And with that thought she simply relaxed into the feeling of awkwardness to discover, to her amazement, that it really was ok, that it didn't have to be any different, that she didn't need to pretend after all.

This is real freedom; freedom that has no prerequisites; freedom *within* whatever is happening.

Although she'd probably heard that message a thousand times before—to go beneath the storyline and feel deeply into the presently arising dis-ease—this time it suddenly hit home experientially and she could taste its power.

And that same movement, to no longer avoid but rather open to the fullness of the immediate experience, is available to us all, whatever our situation. Whether it's feelings of vulnerability, anxiety or shame, thoughts about not being good enough, or the discomfort caused by constant striving to 'fit in'; whether it's the fear of speaking in front of groups, of being laid bare without our carefully crafted layers of personality for protection, or of seeing all our 'certainties' about who we are and what life is, fall apart; whatever it may be that we normally spend our lives trying to avoid or deny, when we dare to drop into the raw, felt experience of those energies, we realise the marvel that who we really are is never threatened.

As our confidence in that recognition grows, as we even start to see beauty in the 'discomfort', wonder in its aliveness, we naturally lose interest in playing the game of avoidance—of needing to anaesthetise ourself with compulsive thinking, working, busyness, gossiping, TV watching, drinking, drug taking or whatever our particular means of escape might be.

Then, just like my friend, in being released from all the extra psychological suffering that is born of life needing to be otherwise, we're free to act naturally and spontaneously, to be playful, creative and connected, to express and celebrate our own uniqueness—we're free to enjoy the party.

One Taste

If we've been attending spiritual groups for some time we may have noticed a frustrating pattern beginning to emerge: in the meetings we might experience all sorts of peaceful, loving, happy and expansive feelings, but as soon as we return to our busy lives it all seems to disappear without a trace and we're left feeling frustrated and confused—often with a growing sense of futility and hopelessness, as to hold onto 'it' seems like such an impossible task. So what is going on?

Whenever we associate our true nature with a particular experience—such as a peaceful, happy, loving feeling—then, since the nature of all experiences are that they come and go, when those feelings inevitably go we immediately imagine we've lost 'it', and off we go in search again. That's the cycle of seeking.

But if the feeling of peace or happiness really is what we truly are, then when that feeling goes we should disappear along with it; but is that what happens, do we suddenly vanish from existence?! No! What we are remains exactly as it is, aware of whatever new feeling is now arising. So *we cannot be made of a particular feeling.*

In fact it's not just feelings that come and go; so too do all the sensations, thoughts, images, sounds, smells and tastes that make up our entire experience, whilst what we are remains the same throughout. So *we cannot be made of any particular experience.*

Since all we can know with our rational mind is experience, and what we truly are is *not* an experience, then if we continue to look in this way it *is* futile and hopeless! Round and round the seeking cycle we go, trying harder and harder to cling onto a particular feeling or sensation, maybe even trying to cultivate a 'blank state'—the mind's version of a non experience!—which, like all states, comes and goes too, until we become so utterly frustrated that we're finally ready to give up completely.

This is an exciting place to be!

For in that giving up we relax the grasping of our 2+2=4 intellectual knowing, and maybe we're ready to courageously free fall beyond the edge of thought, to fully face whatever fear and anxiety may come, and dis-cover an entirely different kind of knowing: a pure, wordless knowing—beyond all descriptions, beyond all understanding—that we can only realise by *being*.

So why do teachers often say that we are love, peace and happiness?

The peace that is talked about is not the *feeling* of peace, it's much deeper than that; it's the peace that comes from the recognition that this pure knowing that we are is utterly imperturbable, even when our life situation may be totally chaotic. The happiness is born of the realisation that what we are needs nothing, is already complete, however much we may seem to lack in our conventional life. And love is the name

given to the understanding that what we are is utterly inseparable from every feature of the entire manifest world.

It's that deep love, peace and happiness, that radiance of pure
knowing, shining in all its glory, that is the 'one taste' equally
present in both our most blissful and most painful moments;
that cannot be lost or found even, since it is the very source
and nature of what we always already *are*.

Monopoly

As kids, my siblings and I would often get together with other children who lived on our street to play the board game Monopoly. Without fail, every game would evoke such wild extremes of behaviour that they strike me now as a wonderful analogy for the human condition. I'll explain!

You come into 'the game' having no clue whatsoever about how to play. Then you take on an identity: you are the top hat, thimble, racing car, boot, Scottie dog, battleship, iron or wheelbarrow. Uncertain and a little bewildered you make your first tentative steps around the board whilst everyone else tells you the rules (although no one seems to agree exactly on what they are).

Slowly you get the hang of it and begin accumulating money, properties, houses and hotels of your own; and this is where the 'fun' begins! For when things are going well you feel special, powerful, self-satisfied and your thoughts are dominated by schemes and strategies for earning more money, getting more properties, for taking over the entire board. But then, as your fortunes start to slide, and you watch your hard earned piles of cash slowly disappear, your feelings quickly morph into tension, frustration, anxiety; into helplessness, self-pity, envy, regret; into anger, hatred, even rage (there was one boy on our street who, when he realised he couldn't win, would flip the board over sending all the money, cards and houses flying and storm out of the room!).

Then there can be a beautiful moment of clarity: you re-cognise that the money and properties are make-believe, that your true identity is not that little token moving round the board, that *it's only a game.*

And this is where the analogy breaks down, for this 'game of life' is not *only* a game, that way leads to pointlessness and nihilism, rather it's a *real* game, and who you truly are *is being all of it:* the board, the tokens, the money, the cards, the houses and hotels, the highs and lows, the successes and disappointments, *the entire experience itself.*

With that glorious realisation the game still plays on—you still have to pay the 'electric company', 'water works' and 'income tax', still experience all the challenges of living—but the heavy seriousness transmutes into a sweet lightness for, whatever happens, *You've already won!* And now the joy is in the *playing.*

PART 4: 2016

Blossoming into Life

In my mid twenties I went to drama school in London and at the end of the course we were to perform the play 'Summerfolk' as a showcase for acting agents. As the day of the first performance approached, our director, who had been looking increasingly frustrated, suddenly stopped the rehearsal and gathered us all together. He told us the play was 'dead' and that he'd finally worked out why.

Since being taken on by a good agent was seen as an important springboard into the acting business, we were all feeling the pressure. As a result, to feel more in control, more safe and secure, we were fixing every detail of our performance— where to stand, where to look, how to move, how to speak each line. That's why it was so lifeless.

So our director pulled the rug from under our feet. He told us that, other than the script itself, he didn't want to see anything he'd seen before. A wave of silent terror spread through the room!

But as we anxiously restarted the play something incredible began to happen. In being stripped of our stale conclusions, in not knowing what anyone else was about to do, suddenly we were naturally deeply listening to one another, responding freely, spontaneously, and in fresh and exciting new ways— magic was happening.

Like flowers that for safety had been hiding tight in their buds, we were daring to risk blossoming into life.

Similarly in our daily experience, to feel more in control, more safe and secure, we too can 'fix our performance'—nailing life down with definitions and beliefs about who we are and the-way-it-is. But in living inside our prison of beliefs then, just like with the play, life can start to seem dull, repetitive and uninspiring.

When we courageously dare to drop our well rehearsed masks, to be exposed in all our nakedness, to openly feel the raw energy of whatever fear, self-doubt or unworthiness that may arise, to be the loving embrace that welcomes it all in, then, in our tender vulnerability, the dividing walls of our mental prison come tumbling down and we rediscover 'aliveness', 'playfulness', 'spontaneity' and 'possibility', along with deep, wordless wonder at this mind-blowing, miraculous happening that is the here and now.

The Real Fireworks

Dear You

Do You actually realise just how incredibly magnificent You are?
How wonderfully marvellously extraordinarily spectacularly GLORIOUS You really really are?!

For it is You, yes YOU, glittering as this ever-fresh kaleidoscope of experiencing,
shimmering as this rich collage of colours, sounds, tastes, textures and smells,
tingling as this vibrant body of sensation,
giving birth to every particle of life from stars, planets, mountains and oceans,
to the sparkling glint of an eye and the quickening of the heart.

Even dreaming up the pretence that You are but a fraction of Your immensity,
that You are unlovable, not enough, not allowed;
that You must attain or achieve in order to be worthy;
oscillating between self-deprecation and self-inflation.

And joyously dis-covering Your true splendour once again—
that *You are love, You are enough, You are allowed,*
that You are of infinite importance,
that Your worth is beyond measure,
that nothing is looking, and nothing is being seen,
that it's all YOU YOU YOU!

Forget 'spiritual fireworks';
the miracle of the 'ordinary' this-here-now is the real firework
display.

But even all that pales into insignificance
compared to Your greatest magic trick of all—
You somehow manage to spontaneously conjure YourSelf
into existence,
out of nothing-at-all!

How amazing is that?

You are an absolute genius!!!

With love from You

The Most Glorious Song of All

I breath in this silent, formless, invisible breath . . . and as it flows out, my vocal cords come alive with vibration, chopping the breath into waves of sound, my head and chest buzzing with resonance, my mouth, tongue and lips sculpting the breath further giving rise to the sound of my voice, singing my song.

And what is this music made of? That same silent, formless, invisible breath, shapeshifting into colourful, intricately detailed tones—it is the sound of silence.

Our true essence is the silent, formless, invisible 'breath' that gives rise to the music of life itself—to an infinite variety of forms, colours, textures and sounds, from the splash of a raindrop to galaxies of stars; to a vast spectrum of feelings, flavours and smells, of thoughts and sensations; to the human story of wholeness splintering into separateness, of feeling like an isolated, fearful, insufficient 'me', of developing a self image and an imitation will to protect our sense of inadequacy from ever being exposed, of the fruitless search for lasting fulfilment and freedom from all our dis-ease. And then there is the great return, when we put all our beliefs, opinions and sophisticated knowledge temporarily aside, and explore the present moment freshly, like a child, as if for the very first time, and re-cognise the magical wonder of our true essence—the silence that *is* the music.

With that sublime dis-covery—that we have nothing to lose or gain even, that we are already whole, already complete—we can finally open to innocence, to tenderness, to vulnerability without closing down or turning away (and if we do we can open to that too). We can finally begin to face *all* of life, and meet *all* that we'd split off from and repressed in the name of survival, welcoming it back home, back into wholeness (welcoming even our inability to welcome).

And with our ever increasing capacity for care and compassion, we naturally begin to move from craving to curiosity, from longing to loving, from seeking to celebrating this remarkable multi-sensorial composition—the most glorious song of all.

Waking Up from Waking Up

It can be incredibly exciting when we first start to 'wake up' to the wonder that, "Yes, I am Presence! I am this Knowing! And yes, experience is not what I ever thought it to be: I don't experience a world of solid, independently existing things; there is an ever fresh flow of colours, sounds, smells and tastes, of sensations, thoughts and feelings arising, that is indivisible from the Knowing of it, that includes the very 'me' I imagined myself to exclusively be! Yes! Yes! Wow!!!"

For me, I was then lucky enough to meet my wife and have children and, in the crucible of family life, have all my still-existing reactivity reflected right back in my face! What a blessing! I was forced to acknowledge that, "Oh, yeah, nothing has changed here, actually; all the old patterns are still running."

And then a beautiful new journey began: of shining the light of that recognition deep into the shadowy, 'hidden' areas of experience; of sincerely wondering, "What beliefs are still being held onto here?" And seeing, "Oh, yes, there it is: abandonment from God, deficiency—I'm not good enough, I'm not worthy, I'm not allowed, I'm unlovable—and shame for that deficiency; sadness, grief for the loss of Wholeness, anger, rage, along with tightness in the head, chest, abdomen, hips, legs, feet; and, what's this? Oh wow, I'm a monster! I'm a diabolical monster that doesn't even deserve to be alive!" And acknowledging it, finally, not wallowing in it or acting it out or trying to get rid of it, but facing it, including it, feeling it, loving it, allowing those voices to finally be heard, to unfurl.

And more than that: the I that I Am, it's not just being James here, it's being that murderer and that paedophile, it's the same 'I' wrapped up in a particular collection of beliefs and ways of operating; opening to that too, that's instant compassion right there. I don't have to accept or support that kind of behaviour, or become a masochist and go seeking that stuff out; it's about acknowledgment, full acknowledgment, not denying and splitting off.

This is a part of the message that I really want to bring forward, because for me it was utterly vital, and still is—still is! These tendencies and clenches in the body are still working their way out, and that's the paradox: this Presence that we deeply are is always already complete, and yet in manifestation there is unending potential for growth and change. It's vital because it's only in fully meeting these denied and repressed patterns and holdings, that they can unfold and release the energy and creativity locked inside—that's transformation.

What can happen is that we have a genuine recognition, but then our pristine, bulletproof philosophy of 'there's no-one here, nothing to do, nothing to get', or whatever dogma we believe in, becomes the new safe place to cling to, to avoid fully facing what's still lurking in the shadows; then there can be no real transformation—we can actually become more in denial, more dishonest than ever before.

That's not meant as an accusation; because when I think back in my own experience, I didn't even realise when I was being dishonest. But in its own time there's a sensitivity that comes, and a courageous dropping of the facades, and we start to really acknowledge just how dishonest we've been. We're not then beating ourself up for that—that's only more of the same nonsense; it's just clarity, it's just being open about what's really going on. There's such beauty in that: more and more clarity, more and more honesty.

That's why I love holding my meetings and retreats: simply being together with a group of people without anyone needing to pretend in any way—not pretending about who we are and trying to present some kind of front, some kind of cleverness, or specialness; but also not pretending spiritually either, that we know something, that 'this is how it is', or worrying about using the 'correct' language or getting it 'right'.

It's just so delicious when we share that deep honesty and openness, when we're simply here, together, with nothing to hold; that's when the divisions fall apart, that's when we know ourself as Love.

For the latest writings, music, books, free videos
and upcoming online courses from James
visit:

www.jameseaton.org

For community & support, join James's Facebook group:

'James Eaton Community and Support Group'

UPCOMING ONLINE COURSES

COURSE 1: SELF REALISATION

Am I exclusively a separate subject, moving through a world of independently existing objects and other subjects?

When we look afresh, with childlike innocence, we can experience ourself in an entirely new way.

COURSE 2: LIFE TRANSFORMATION

Is Self-realisation the 'end goal' or the beginning of a beautiful process of unravelling?

When we deeply listen to the body and mind, we can begin to acknowledge the self-beliefs, body tensions and coping mechanisms that still persist, allowing them to gently unfold and so unlock the energy and creativity bound therein.

COURSE 3: MODELS OF REALITY

Does scientific materialism—that it's 'particles all the way down'—really bear true to our actual experience?

First we explore the process of conceptualising, before going beyond all models completely—the ultimate reset. Then, taking our *total* experience into account, we put together a new model of reality that *includes* the powerful discoveries of science, whilst freeing us from its limitations, serving to both inspire and empower.

About the Author

James Eaton graduated in Maths from Oxford University, then tried a number of vocations, including working as a singer-songwriter, an actor, and a school teacher in inner city London. Despite achieving success, he couldn't shift a profound sense of lack and longing. What followed was an intense spiritual search that culminated in directly realising the wholeness of being—the home he'd been longing for.

Since 2011 James has been leading workshops and retreats internationally, guiding others to that same realisation, and to the subsequent life transformation and empowerment it can offer. He lives in Totnes, UK, with his wife, Eleonora, and their two sons, Edward and Ludo.

jameseaton.org
Facebook
Instagram: @jameseaton_org
Twitter: @jameseaton_org

Printed in Great Britain
by Amazon